# POLITICS OF HOPE

---

## *A Failed Strategy*

---

**Tom Caiazzo**

**University Press of America,® Inc.**
Lanham · Boulder · New York · Toronto · Plymouth, UK

Copyright © 2007 by
University Press of America,® Inc.
4501 Forbes Boulevard
Suite 200
Lanham, Maryland 20706
UPA Acquisitions Department (301) 459-3366

Estover Road
Plymouth PL6 7PY
United Kingdom

Library of Congress Control Number: 2007922245
ISBN-13: 978-0-7618-3728-2 (paperback : alk. paper)
ISBN-10: 0-7618-3728-0 (paperback : alk. paper)

⊖™ The paper used in this publication meets the minimum
requirements of American National Standard for Information
Sciences—Permanence of Paper for Printed Library Materials,
ANSI Z39.48—1984

# Contents

# Acknowledgements

This project would not have been possible without the support of many people. I want to first thank all of the people who supported my campaign for office. I am especially grateful for the hard work and support of Mary Matusik and her family, Daryl Irland, Chuck LaLanne, Josh Andor, Tiam Tavokoli, Champ Teng, Jennie and Jeff Irland, Dr. Cary Israel, Mark Hultgren, Judge John Payton, Eric Donihoo, Kevin Henard, Greg Dennis and his family, Marty Berryman and his family, Tony Airhart, and John "Zonk" Lanzillo, Jr. Without their friend-ship, guidance, and support, there would be no book to write. I want to also thank University Press of America for publishing this book, and Louisa Goodwill for her editing expertise. And finally, thanks to my wife Janet, son Dante, parents, brothers, cousins, and numerous friends who endured this long process with me, and always offered support and love. May God bless each and every one of you.

# Introduction

It's been roughly four years since I was beat at the ballot box running for the U.S. Congress. By now, one would assume that my campaign to run again is in full-gear. The lessons learned and the education attained would be an advantage for my second attempt. Yet, though the energy and interest still burns, I am categorically and unequivocally disappointed. Saddened because I still can't seem to understand why so few people participate in the political process.

Having now taught political science for the past fifteen years in both the university and community college setting, I had "enough" in 2001. From the career politicians to the expanding national debt, it became a challenge to even watch the evening news. I was also tired of hearing from both the young and old that our system "stinks" and that "we can't make a difference." This feeling was especially true among the literally thousands of students I had taught over the years.

The apathy and ignorance among our college-aged population is at an all time high. Students are also frustrated with politics as usual. They don't trust elected officials. They feel that they can't make a difference, and believe that their vote doesn't count. As a community leader, educator, and political science scholar, it became my personal crusade and responsibility to eliminate this dangerous pattern.

After getting the approval from my family, I decided to run for political office. Granted that I knew my chances of electoral success were slim to none, the attempt was more important than the results. I had to prove to these students (and people) that I will start "practicing what I was preaching." I would be the vehicle that could channel all the dissatisfaction and discontent into positive civic action. I would be the candidate of "hope" for the sake of our political system.

I also concluded that the office to seek would be the one that could make the largest impact with my objective, the United States Congress. Conceptualize this: a political science professor and political novice defeat a career incumbent. The victory motivates those who thought they never had a chance. Thousands are influenced by this effort. People, especially the young, would become more aware and informed. Civic engagement and involvement would propel to record highs. The "American Dream" would indeed be alive!

Though my family and Inner-Circle supported this challenge, many people thought it was "political suicide." The congressman I was trying to defeat was career incumbent, Sam Johnson. The Republican from District 3 (North Dallas suburbs) was a staunch conservative and a former-POW. Regardless of the fact that, in my opinion, he wasn't an active or aggressive legislator, Sam Johnson was nonetheless a political hero. Due to his disability and service, people would literally "cry" when he would show-up at a community event.

My candidacy was quickly dismissed as an election for "name recognition" or simply about "ego." The so-called "experts" in the community didn't have a clue. In fact, I liked the odds even better. This was "the race" and "the candidate" that I needed and I wanted to help revive the damaged spirits of the electorate.

My electoral strategy was simple: defeat the incumbent in the primary by capitalizing on the 95% of registered voters that didn't vote. Yes, only 4-6% of registered voters actually participated in the Republican primary! Prior elections also had the incumbent uncontested in the primary.

I knew by the scope of the vote, I was going to get 1% no matter what. Now, I only needed ten percent of the 90% that didn't vote to turn-out in my favor and guarantee me victory. My correct estimates quantitatively proved that only around 15,000 people would vote in the primary, and thus I only needed 7,501 votes to be the next congressman. How hard could that be? Likewise, studies showed that most people never heard of their congressman. So, if I worked hard I would be a shoe-in.

I would also target a plethora of "groups" who would vote for me regardless of my opponent: students and educators, racial and ethnic minorities, and the non-voters. The incumbent had done little to help any of these groups that I genuinely supported, especially students and educators. With the latter, he did nil about increasing their pell grants, providing federal funding to the local Collin County Community College (my place of employment), and to assist education across the board. Similarly, how could any elementary, secondary, or college educator not vote for one of their own? Again, I ONLY needed another 10% to guarantee a win!

To "target" these groups, conventional and unconventional grassroots activities were organized on a limited budget: voter registration drives, "Rock the Vote" concerts, entering community parades, door-to-door campaigning, professional wrestling fundraisers, dating games, athletic challenges, etc. I also erected a giant 6' x 6' campaign sign to the back of my Dodge pickup truck where people would see me coming from a ¼ mile down the road. Entertainment, music, food, and fun were always the central theme.

I would also target the few but growing racial and ethnic minority groups that had been ostracized by the conservative incumbent. The Asian, Hispanic, Indian, and African American community were at the forefront. In the aggregate, this plan would surely generate some of the many who were discontent.

After meeting with my Inner-Circle (a collection of friends who were also disgruntled with the politics-as-usual scene) my next endeavor was to meet with the Republican Party leadership. To my chagrin, the reception was less than favorable. Not only did Buddy Ragdley, (the Collin County Republican Party Chairman) discourage me from running, he even questioned my integrity. Likewise, at future party events, a plethora of the "old-guard" in the party would treat me as though I had the plague. The treatment was down-right insulting, offensive, and shameful. Some comments: "How dare I challenge Sam?;" "Who does he think he is?;" and, "Doesn't he know what "Sam" means to this community?" My campaign treasurer was even told that my candidacy was "political suicide." I thought "have they no sense of decency?"

If it wasn't for the county party secretary, I doubt that I would have even received all the important paperwork and information needed to run for U.S. Congress. Though a lot of the information is available online, any local help was deeply appreciated. Even though I knew the Secretary herself would never have voted for me, I thanked her for the support. I also had some "back-door" help from some Republicans who felt that my treatment by the party leadership was reprehensible.

The filing fee to run for U.S. Congress was $1,500. If I garnered enough signatures (500), that fee would be waived. Since I only raised roughly $12,000 for my entire campaign run, compared to my opponents nearly one million dollars, I did just that. In fact, I was the first candidate in the area to run for U.S. Congress to not pay a filing fee. The incumbent didn't even try to get the signatures and rather opted to pay the filing fee! This made me feel good. I knew I had at least 500 votes—the required number of signatures to get on the ballot and get the filing fee waived.

I also decided to meet with the county chairman of the Democratic Party. Though the party has been unsuccessful in the region, they still had around 2,000 people vote in the primary for uncontested races. In a cautious and diplomatic manner, I tried to solicit a "cross-over" voting behavior from the Democrats. In this case, I would ask registered Democrats to "cross-over" and vote Republican (at least for me) in the open primary.

The return would be access, something they presently don't and never had from the incumbent. I would at least hear and address the concerns of the Democrats. If I won, I also promised to appoint a few Democrats to positions of leadership to govern in a more bi-partisan manner. Unfortunately, I failed in this effort. The Democrats still don't have any access and their concerns aren't being addressed.

And then 9/11/2001 happened. Let the campaign begin.

Everything I write in this book isn't fabricated or untrue. I take full responsibility for the content and make no apologies for what you will read. The material that follows will not be sugar-coated. I will tell it like it is and reveal all the intimate efforts of my political campaign. And, out of respect for privacy, I will only use one pseudonym for a major political player that I encountered during the campaign. I am sure the personal shame he feels on a daily basis is punishment enough.

Our great Republic depends upon people participating and being civically engaged at all levels. If I can inspire or motivate one person to run for political office to make a significant difference, then I have accomplished my goal. Though Shakespeare may have been right when he said that the only thing people care about is "bread and circuses," I say otherwise. People need a reason to put down the bread and quit going to the circus. I made the effort but implemented a failed strategy. It is now your turn. This time, however, learn from my miscues and do it right.

# Born on 9/11

I was born on 9/11/1966 in the Bronx (NY). I am the 2nd of four brothers to my Mom (Lena) and Father (Felice). My father was born in Pomigliano D'Arco, Italy and my mother in the Bronx. As a first-generation Italian-American, my family worked hard to make sure that everyone had an opportunity to achieve. In his twenties, my father legally arrived in New York City "fresh off the boat" with literally nothing. He worked diligently to progress and get ahead and didn't ask for preferential treatment. He worked a variety of construction jobs until he became a foreman with the local construction union.

My mother worked very hard in her teens and early twenties doing a variety of secretarial and retail jobs. When married, she stayed at home and raised my older brother (Angelo) and me. Unlike my father who is strict, my mother is the most sensitive woman I know. The love and care she provided, as well as the concern to keep us shielded from a temperate father, is enormous.

I was raised in an old-fashioned Italian manner. My mother stayed home and raised her two sons. My father was the authoritarian patriarch but would do anything for his family. Seeking a better life and financial gain, my parents relocated to Florida in 1974. It was a major risk, not to mention that my brother John was born the same year. Taking up a new career as a restaurateur, my father settled the family in the city of Orlando.

The neighborhood was predominately lower, middle-class and everyone was very friendly. My brother Angelo and I were bused from a predominately all-white neighborhood to a black school district—some forty-five minutes away. We attended Eccelston Elementary in the Ivey Lane district. Though my parents were apprehensive, they had no choice because of the new federal and state laws.

To be honest, I really enjoyed my Elementary school years. My brother and I had no problem with attending a majority-black school. We made friends, played sports together, and were treated like all the other kids.

We were also disciplined in the same manner. My brother and I would often be in Principal Rawls' office for a paddling with the other kids. One time, I remember Mr. Rawls lined-up about seven of us. I was the youngest and thus put at the end of the line. Mr. Rawls began to give each their "10 licks." I was somehow placed on the end and always got two extra.

I believe this early experience in my life had a positive impact to how I view racial and ethnic minorities. I see people for who they are, not the color of their skin. Some of my best friends throughout my life and even to this day are African Americans.

A few years later, my father decided to sell his pizza restaurant in Orlando and open another one about one-hour south in the pastoral town of St. Cloud. My brother and I were enrolled in St. Cloud Middle School. It was a decent school but a bit more rural. The school was somewhat segregated and their behavior seemed more country. It was here that I was introduced to chewing tobacco, snuff, cowboy boots and hats, rodeo, and other southern things that I found odd. Due to the massive growth of Central Florida over the next few years, thankfully, the area would become much more diverse.

After school, my brother and I would rotate days and work in the restaurant—we hated it. I also disliked school. I liked the people and social interaction, but not the academics. I wanted to be a professional football player. I loved the Los Angeles Rams and saw myself playing for them in the near future. I studied very little and could care less about most subjects. My reading was also below average.

I will never forget my mother and me meeting with Mr. Fawbush. Mr. Fawbush was the principal of St. Cloud Middle School. He explained to my Mom that my reading was bad and that she had to get me to read more at home. Mr. Fawbush said, "Tom, what do you like to read?" In front of my mother and feeling embarrassed, I said: "professional football and wrestling magazines." As my Mom cringed, Mr. Fawbush surprised me when he said, "Mrs. Caiazzo, it really doesn't matter what he reads, as long as he is reading. Get him to read as much as he can and eventually his reading will improve. He will also start reading other things. As his reading improves, so will his writing and speaking skills." I never had any problems with speaking, but writing is another story. Thank you Mr. Fawbush!

My youngest brother Philip was born around this time. Philip was born deaf. I love Philip so much and seemed to bond with him more than my other brothers. We were inseparable. Philip and I would often play "two on two" football against Angelo and John. Philip would run like a gazelle past John and pull in my forty yard bomb pass. When I ran for office in 2002, I made sure to address the needs of the deaf community.

It was at St. Cloud High School that I became interested in politics. In Mr. Landrum's AP History class, we often discussed current political events. The class was very active and Mr. Landrum is a great teacher. I remember often debating with Jennifer Woods, Jennifer Castro, and Martin Roman.

I was also very close with the racial and ethnic minorities at the school. There was Gabe Hunter, Billy Hamilton, Vince Eady, Mike Wiggins, and Andre Barrington. We had great times together. I personally witnessed and know they experienced covert and overt discrimination and racism at school and in the community. It was embarrassing, but I made sure that I treated them equally and with respect.

Though neither of my parents was civically engaged, I was pushed by my father to strive to become a lawyer. I wasn't sure about becoming a lawyer, but I always noticed that most lawyers who came into the restaurant were always talking politics. I loved social studies, especially geography. But I was intrigued by the political process. I often joked about becoming President of the United States or a Supreme Court Justice.

During this time, the United States was in an arms race with the Soviet Union. The president was Ronald Regan and I really liked his approach. President Reagan talked tough and vowed to back it up. He also seemed very genuine and spoke from his heart. In November of 1984, I was eligible to vote in my first election. I proudly cast my vote for President Reagan. And then I met Dan Parker.

Mr. Parker was my dual-enrollment economics teacher. He was also running for the Supervisor of Elections position. Dan is a passionate man and really inspired me about the political system. He also has a wonderful wife, Candace, who was my middle school English teacher. I was also good friends with their daughter. So, at 17 years old, I immediately joined his campaign and did what I could to help him win. I made phone calls, put together and placed out campaign signs, passed out literature, etc. Though he lost the election, it was my first taste of the political campaign process.

During my senior year, I signed-up with the U.S. Army. Along with a couple of my buddies (Vince "Bobo" Eady and Martin Roman) we decided that St. Cloud offered us no hope. I also didn't want to go to college right away nor work at the family restaurant. I was working part-time at McDonalds, and saw no future there. So, under the agreement that I would go in at the rank of an E-3 (Private first-class), I was upset when a few of my friends who went in before me didn't get the rank and pay promise. The recruiter deceived my friends. After this, I made sure that he wasn't going to get over on me. With the help of my congressman, Bill Nielson, I got out of my contract.

A few weeks later, I decided to join the Air Force. With my parents taken aback, I left for Lackland Air Force base in San Antonio two days after walking into the recruiter's office. After getting my head shaved and spending three trying weeks in boot-camp, I applied for and received an Entry Level separation. The reason: being misled by the recruiter.

With a bald cranium and no options, I returned to the family business. I decided that it was time to go to college. With the ambition to play college football, I was offered a tryout as a quarterback at Central Methodist University (then College) in Fayette (MO). I had never met Coach Larry Anderson. He was recommended to me by friend and former New York Giant, Joe Morrison. Coach Morrison was the Head football coach at the University of New Mexico. Though it was my dream to play for him, I was no where near ready for the NCAA one level. He recommended that I contact Coach Anderson. Central Methodist was an NAIA program, and this level would give me a chance to get acclimated with the offense and get in football shape.

After a positive tryout with Coach Anderson he offered me a scholarship. Coach said I had a "quick release like Dan Marino," and he gave me the playbook to study (I still have the playbook). I would be assigned to the Junior Varsity team during summer practice, and then the rest would be up to me. Before I left campus, I met with my academic advisor and declared Geography as my major. I also organized my class schedule for the upcoming fall semester, and completed all other relevant paperwork for admissions.

Unfortunately, the scholarship wasn't a full-ride. I still had to come up with some $10,000 more to cover the private school's yearly tuition, board and fees. When I asked my father to pay for this expense, he refused. At the time I was furious and thought he was holding me back from my dream of playing in the NFL. I entered into a state of both depression and rage.

Out of respect, I unhappily called Coach Anderson and explained the situation. In retrospect, at 5'8" and weighing 185lbs, I think my father made the right decision. Then again, come every football season, sometimes I think he didn't.

After pouting for a few weeks, I decided to get myself together and move forward. There was no way I was going to continue working for my Dad, especially after the way he handled the Central Methodist decision. Since I loved to travel and have always been fascinated with the airline industry, I decided to become a Travel Agent.

I enrolled at ACT Travel School in Pompano Beach (FL). My parents supported this idea. I am not sure if they agreed with this decision because of the Central Methodist situation and/or because I had enough money to pay for the school on my own. Nonetheless in the summer of 1986, after 2 months of off-campus independent study and one-month on campus training, I completed my program and graduated with a Certificate in Travel Studies. Upon graduation, though I was promised placement, I had no job opportunities.

The experience at ACT Travel secured my quest for higher education. ACT Travel School was an unaccredited institution and I basically got ripped off. After spending some $4,000 at this school, in the end I got nothing. It was at this time I vowed to "wake-up." If I was going to get ahead, it was time to do it right and attend college and get a "real" education.

After a few months working part-time for Florida Express Airlines Air New Orleans, and a few other jobs, I relocated to Miami (FL). During travel school I met a young lady, Esther Minay, who became my girlfriend for more than a year. Through her, I met Stanley Lo, who was a Station manger for Continental Airlines. He hired me and I stayed there on and off for more than a year. I started out as a Ramp Agent and moved up to Lead Agent (working the ticket counter and gate).

I also enrolled full-time at Miami Dade Community College. Though I was a part-time employee, I would often work more than 40+ hours a week. A typical day would range from getting up at 6:30am and completing class around 1:00pm. I would then go home, get a bite to eat, and then be at work around 3:00pm. My day would conclude around 11:00pm.

In mid-1987 Eastern, Frontier, and New York Air filed for bankruptcy. Under its rogue Chairman, Frank Lorenzo, Continental purchased each airline and took over most of their routes. It was at this time I was asked to relocate to Denver and be a full-time Lead Agent.

At 21 years old, I was offered an opportunity to be one of the youngest Lead Agents in the business. I was good and could always make an irate passenger smile. My pay of $6.80 an hour was going to increase to a little more than $10. Yet, I turned down the position. In fact, because I got so much heat from everyone because of my rejection, I eventually quit Continental altogether.

Why? Well, it had nothing to do with my girlfriend because by this time we already split. The reason is simply that I was finally settled into school. I enjoyed going to college and had made a bunch of great friends. I was engaged at the institution and in the community. I was learning so much from my professors such as Micel de Benedictis, Biagio Auricchio, and Adrienne Goldstein. For the first time in my life, I felt that I was doing the right thing. And I was doing it pretty-much on my own.

So, I quit a full-time career opportunity to finish college. I was told by many that it was a bad move. I didn't think so. I had some money in the bank and worked as a Waiter for Chang Catering and took a few other side jobs to pay the bills. In retrospect, it was the best decision I ever made. A few years later, Continental went bankrupt and laid-off many people. I know lots of men and women who lost everything.

In April of 1987, I graduated from Miami Dade Community College with my Associate of Arts degree. I didn't attend the ceremony and that really irritated my parents, especially my father. It wasn't until a few years later that I realized graduation ceremonies aren't for you, but for your family. I wouldn't make that mistake again.

Prior to graduation, I applied for admission to Western Carolina University in Cullowhee (NC). My family opened a restaurant and small hotel in a nearby town, Sylva. I disliked the area from the time I got there. Besides the constant bickering with my father, the place was no energetic and sunny Florida. After about two weeks, I moved backed to St. Cloud and enrolled for the second summer session at the University of Central Florida.

Though the discipline of Geography was my dream major, UCF didn't offer that program. So, I decided to declare Political Science my major. I was going to focus on the International Relations and Comparative Politics area—because of the Geography offerings. I commuted one hour every day and got a part-time job as a Travel Agent at Osceola Travel in Kissimmee (FL). The commute was tough but I was on a mission. I also enrolled in Dr. Henry Kennedy's Canadian Studies class.

Dr. Kennedy was an eloquent speaker and conducted himself as a professional in and out of the classroom. When he spoke I couldn't help but absorb every word that left his mouth. He also did something that very few in my college career had done: he inspired me!

I want to go on record and say that Dr. Kennedy was the best professor I had the honor to both be a student of and know as a colleague. He was my mentor and gave me advice about the profession and life. Dr. Kennedy is the person who helped me become a serious scholar.

I also met Eugene "Torchy" Clark. He was my physical education instructor. He is also a legendary basketball coach and was recently inducted in the Florida Sports Hall of Fame. We used to talk basketball all the time and he even influenced me to get into basketball officiating. I teetered with the idea of being a high school government teacher and basketball coach, but for some reason I never pursued it. We also talked politics and I loved to listen to him prioritize life which I still follow today: 1) God, 2) Family, 3) Health, 4) Education/Job, and 5) Friends/Social Activities.

I graduated in August of 1989 with my B.A. degree in Political Science, and this time I attended the ceremony. My parents were very happy and proud. I thanked many of the professors who were in attendance who inspired me such as Dr. Crepeau, Dr. Davidson, Professor Gergley, and of course, Dr. Kennedy.

I was the first person in my family to graduate college. In fact, on my father's side, I was the first and on my mother's side the second. I remember the graduation meal at the 94th Aero Squadron Steak House with my family. Even my boss, Ted Boburka, was there. That night, I ate a big porterhouse steak along with about five loafs of their specialty bread.

Upon graduation I had a few job opportunities, but none really stood out. I spent the next few months going to job interviews and not accepting their offers. I was also hanging out a lot with my friends, especially Jeff Scalli. Jeff is about ten years older than me and is a great friend. He was always there for me when things at school seemed improbable. We had lots of fun together. I recall raiding the cafeteria at his employment after hours while watching professional wrestling pay-per-views on the company's giant screen TV.

With really no job offers that stood out, I decided to visit with Dr. Kennedy. Upon his advice, I decided to apply to graduate school. With the guidance and support of Dr. Kennedy, I enrolled back at UCF as a Post-Baccalaureate student and enrolled in nine semester graduate hours in political science.

Before leaving campus, I met with Professor Clark. We spoke and he suggested that I go to graduate school and become a college basketball graduate assistant. I applied to Lehigh University in Bethlehem (PA). Though it wasn't Florida, I couldn't have selected a more ideal place. It was located near Uncle Tony and Aunt Anna's house. Their four children, Angelo, Ralph, Joey, and Carmella, are my closest cousins.

Over the years of visiting the Lehigh Valley, I made great friends in the area such as Sabadine, Sonny, and Koach. I envisioned Ralph and me going to the Pocono Mountains to party on the weekend in his Porsche. So, if I was fortunate to get the assistantship, things would have been great.

As I waited word from Lehigh, I was getting ready for graduate school at UCF. A few weeks passed and I received a generic rejection letter from both the Lehigh political science department and basketball coach. I was angry and immaturely wrote a letter back to both stating basically that they made a bad decision. In a way, I was also relived because now I knew exactly what I had to do.

I decided to move into my own apartment across from the UCF campus. With the heavy research load, there was no way that I was going to commute back and forth to school. So, with my parents help, I rented a one bedroom apartment at the University Villas for $335 a month. Though it wasn't the best place, it would accomplish my objective. Along with my buddy Warren Noyes, I remember one hot summer day the two of us hanging-out in my apartment. He was raising a storm because I wouldn't run the air conditioning. I was on a tight budget and really only slept and showered there anyway. Most of the time, I was on campus studying, attending class, or working.

Speaking of working, I also secured a part time job at the UCF Police Department with the Parking and Traffic Division as a Parking Patroller. In short, I was the guy who would write you a ticket if you inappropriately parked on campus. I loved that job. I worked very little and got paid more than $6.00 an hour. Most of the time, I would study in the library or shoot basketball in the gym. I will never forget the Director, Ina Carpenter and her assistant, Shirley. Everyone treated me with respect and supported my graduate studies.

It was also at the UCF Police Department that I met the love of my life and now wife, Janet. To be honest, in 1990, a steady relationship was the furthest thing from my mind. I was a graduate student and enjoying the college atmosphere. One day when I was loafing on the job, I happened to bump into Janet. Call it destiny, but when I saw her it was like I was hit by a bolt of lightning. In fact, it seemed as though I couldn't look at her too long because I was blinded by her beauty. It was unreal. In short, we would soon date and marry a year or so later.

After successfully passing the nine hours with an "A" and two "Bs," I was accepted outright into the M.A. political science program. It was during this time that I started to get involved with political campaigns. I also started my own political party, the Renaissance Party.

Like many folks, I was disgusted with politics-as-usual from both political parties. So I offered an alternative. Though it attained local media coverage, it drew little support. I remember an interview on the "Clive Thomas" radio show. The local ABC affiliate Channel 9 also did a three minute cover story on the party. My studies required a lot more attention than I could devote to the party. Though Anthony Ginisi aligned with the party when he unsuccessfully ran for Mayor of Orlando in 1990, it eventually disbanded.

I had some interesting professors in my graduate program. Besides Dr. Kennedy, I really liked Dr. Robert Bledsoe, Dr. Philip Pollock, Dr. Johnson-Freeze, and Dr. Mark Stern. They were all very demanding and there were days that I often wondered if I could satisfy their research requirements. Yet, in the end, their objectives made me a scholar.

Dr. Joan Johnson-Freeze raised my confidence to another level. I never missed a class or an opportunity to answer and/or pose questions in her classes. And, she loved to call on me. I will never forget when Dr. Johnson-Freeze critiqued my oral presentation on the NASP (National Aerospace Plane) with the highest of accolades. She was the best!

In May of 1991, I graduated with my M.A. degree in Political Science. It was a great ceremony and my parents were once again proud. After graduation, I secured a part-time (adjunct) teaching position at the local Valencia Community College (Orlando). I wasn't sure that I was going to be a professor, but Dr. Kennedy and Dr. Johnson-Freeze said I was a natural for the position. I contemplated law school and even took the Law School Admissions Test (LSAT). Regardless, I knew that I had a passion for political science and needed to find my niche in the discipline.

Since it was only teaching two classes, I secured a couple of side jobs to make extra money. I worked as a security guard, basketball official, and substitute teacher. The only school I substitute taught at was Poinciana High School in Poinciana (FL). The school was about 45 minutes from my apartment, so I had no problem commuting to get the experience. Ironically, guess who was the vice-principal? Dan Parker! Some seven years after helping him run for political office, we met again.

My life was now in full bloom but I still had the desire to do more. Law school was on the top of my list, but a few of my friends such as Warren Noyes hated law school. They only wanted to be lawyers for the money. When I started college I vowed never to pursue a career because of the money. If I wanted money I could have stayed in the restaurant business. I wanted a career where I would be happy and wanted to get up and go to work every morning.

As fate would have it, while I was substitute teaching, I happened to look down on the desk calendar and read a quote which vindicated my career approach: "Find a job you love, and you will never work a day in your life." It was at that time I decided to pursue a career as a full-time political science professor. I submitted applications all over Central Florida and waited patiently. I even went back to UCF to get additional graduate hours.

I registered as a delegate for the 1992 Jerry Brown presidential campaign. Though he was a Democrat and me a registered Republican, I really liked his progressive ideas for domestic policy. I agreed with him that not enough was being done for the middle-class. That our education system needed reform and we had to get health care under control. Jerry Brown didn't get the party's nomination. I proudly voted for Bill Clinton in the 1992 presidential election.

Let me say that I have never voted for and will never vote for anyone because of their party affiliation. That is very naive and reckless. To me, the party banner is just a cosmetic label based on where you live. I always vote for the candidate based on how they stand on the issues. This is what a responsible voter should always do.

I was very civically engaged in my community. From grassroots activities to state and federal campaigns, I really enjoyed the political process. Though I was never part of a candidate's inner-circle, I was consumed with the issues and how one voted. I did a plethora of research and always had my facts in line. I even became a major civil libertarian organizing the William Penn Defense League (WPDL).

The WPDL was an organization committed to religious freedom. As a Christian, I think prayer is very important and it has personally affected my life. But I am also tolerant and respectful of others and their religious or non-religious beliefs.

At the time, I organized the first ever Easter "Sunrise Prayer" service in the entire state of Florida. To exercise religious freedom and tolerance, area church and religious leaders would say some words and give a prayer at the lakefront. Even though the Southern Baptist minister embarrassingly spouted out a diatribe pontificating that his religion was the "right one" and everybody else was "going to hell," the event was exceptional.

Though my civic engagement was at an all time high, I still yearned to learn more about the political system. After working part-time for two years at Valencia Community College, it seemed that getting a full-time position without a Ph.D. was impossible. After conversing with Janet and my family, I applied to three doctoral programs—University of Florida, Florida State University, and Clark Atlanta University. I was accepted into Clark Atlanta University's Political Science Doctoral program.

I was so excited to be part of an institution with such great academics and history. It has one of the best civil liberties and rights curriculums in the country. When I visited the campus, everyone from the professors to the campus police treated me with respect. I was very impressed with everything that Clark Atlanta University (CAU) offered.

I relocated to Atlanta and rented a one bedroom apartment two blocks from the Georgia Dome. I loved the urban lifestyle. I walked everywhere and took the MARTA rail system all over Atlanta. During this time, the Atlanta Falcons football team was horrible. I used to wake up Sunday mornings during football season and find free tickets on my truck window. I saw many games that season for free; including my Rams beating the Falcons in a nearly empty stadium.

My wife, Janet, stayed in St. Cloud. We saw each other on the weekends. One weekend I flew home and the other she flew to Atlanta. We did that for almost one academic year. Relocation for Janet was a big decision. She had a full-time job as a law enforcement officer with the UCF Police Department and was destined for promotion and a fabulous career. We also had a nice house and liked the Florida climate and lifestyle. Fortunate for me, she eventually followed her heart and moved with me to Atlanta.

I wanted to continue my teaching career and experience. Since Clark Atlanta University already had all its graduate teaching assistants' set-up for that academic year, I contacted the area local universities and community colleges for employment. Dr. Willoughby Jarrell, the Chair of the Political Science Department at Kennesaw State College (now University), offered me a part time job that fit my schedule.

I appreciate Dr. Jarrell for not only the job opportunity, but all her direction, guidance, and wisdom. She helped me with my instructional methods and the use of effective pedagogy in the classroom. I thank her for the letters of recommendation and her influence with my career.

Moreover, in all my college years, my first semester at CAU was the "hardest." The reading and writing requirements were seen as excessive. The department also demanded participation in and out of class. Granted I loved the interaction, but the course workload about "killed" me!! I often remember asking myself "why" as I read some 500+ pages per week for just my one Urban Studies class with Dr. Bailey.

I completed my first semester with a 3.6 GPA. My only "B" that semester was in my Government and Politics in Modern Africa class with Dr. Guy Martin. It was the only "B" I would get throughout my entire Ph.D. program. Even to this day, that grade bothers me. Not only did it ruin my 4.0, but I believe Dr. Martin gave me that grade in a capricious manner. When I questioned the grade, he said, "Your paper on the war and conditions in Somalia was good, but you relied on a poor source for most of your material." The next semester, this "poor source," *Africa Betrayed* by George B.N. Ayittey, was on Professor Martin's required reading list.

After my first year at CAU, I applied for and was granted a teaching assistantship. This meant free tuition and pay in exchange for teaching two classes. It was a great opportunity and I took full advantage. I taught two sections of introductory political science courses.

Though the academic work was immense, I was challenged and learned a lot from all my instructors. I specialized in four areas of political science: American Government and Public Policy; Political Methodology and Theory; International Relations; and, Urban Politics. I had many great instructors, but the ones who encouraged and motivated me were: Dr. Bennison DeJanes, Dr. Hashim Gibrill; Dr. Michael Bailey; Dr. Robert Fishman; and, Dr. William Boone. Along with Dr. Gretchen McLaughlin, Dr. Boone and Dr. Fishman were on my dissertation committee.

Dr. Boone was another political science professor that inspired me. Like Dr. Kennedy, Dr. Boone is a fantastic person and genuine scholar. But the instructional methods Dr. Boone employed are beyond comparison. Dr. Boone incorporated the Socratic method of instruction and engaged the class accordingly. He would challenge me to think critically and demanded logical answers. He expected individual accountability and responsibility, and was a stickler on the rules and procedures.

I would have to say that Dr. Boone had the most influence in my college education as it pertains to my instruction. I co-opted his instructional methods. The knowledge gained from his classes is immense. Dr. Kennedy was the one who started my educational journey, but Dr. Boone took it to another level.

It was during this time I became very active in the United We Stand America movement. In 1992, Ross Perot ran for President of the United States as an Independent candidate. Though he lost the election, he received almost 19% of the popular vote but no electors. This made Perot the most successful third-party presidential candidate in terms of the popular vote since Theodore Roosevelt's unsuccessful Progressive (Bull Moose) endeavor in the 1912 presidential election.

It was now 1994 and Perot was in full-gear to run again for president in the upcoming 1996 election. As a third party scholar, I had to get involved with this movement for both academic and personal reasons. I was accepted with open arms by Dick Taylor, the Georgia State Director of United We Stand America. I spent hours and days in that office doing research and volunteer work. The organization appreciated my efforts and gave me a scholarship to fund my doctoral dissertation.

I met Ross Perot at a rally in Atlanta. Due to my connections, I had front row seats. Two of my friends from the doctoral program, Oliver Jones and Fred McBride, were my guests. It was a wild rally with lots of one-liners and patriotic songs. Even to this day me and Oliver, who is now a Professor of Political Science at Palo Alto College, San Antonio (TX), banter about the time we had at the event.

I completed my required courses and passed my comprehensive exams in the spring semester of 1995. I was approved for my dissertation, "Third Party Politics and Its Impact on the U.S. Presidency: An Analysis of the George Wallace, John Anderson, and Ross Perot Campaigns and Its Implications for Voter

Dealignment." To this day, I have primary research from all three third party presidential candidates. I have written and presented papers on these findings.

Speaking of Perot, due to historical dualism, our political culture, and the many institutional barriers in place to deter third parties and candidates, I knew from the start that he never had a chance. In late 1994, he decided to again run for President. This time, he found the Reform Party and won their nomination for 1996 presidential election. He lost again and this time only received roughly eight percent of the popular vote and no electors. It's a shame, because I think a multi-party system would be good for our political system, especially with re-spect to voter turnout.

In May of 1995, I attained ABD (all but dissertation) status. I decided it was time to secure a full-time instructional position. Some of my other classmates felt uncomfortable leaving the Atlanta area until their dissertation was complete. They recommended that I also stay. Since I valued their input, I invited some of my closest friends to lunch at our favorite Chinese restaurant near campus.

It was there that I told Trica Headen, Marvin Johnson, Fred McBride, and Oliver Jones of my plans. After outlining my goals, they supported my decision. Though I would be missed, they agreed that I was far enough in my dissertation to complete it wherever I secured employment. More importantly, my dissertation committee agreed that my dissertation was right on track. They ad-vised that I could put the last touches on the rest of it off campus.

I updated my resume and sent out about twenty letters of application. I re-ceived phone interviews from about five, and was invited for an on-campus interview from three: Collin County Community College (Plano, TX), Cuyahoga Community College (Cleveland, Ohio), and South Texas Community College (McAllen, TX). The first interview was at CCCC. I didn't like the area that much—dry, flat, and plain. But the campus was out of this world. The Dean, Harriet Swartz, and the Chair of the Search Committee, Dr. Lynn Jones treated me with the utmost professionalism.

I gave a presentation and answered questions. One faculty member, Ted Lewis tried to fluster me with superficial queries. Another, Dr. David Garrison, tried to throw me off by reading the newspaper and dozing off during my lec-ture. Still, I went back to Atlanta knowing that the job was mine if I wanted it. I felt that confident. Dr. Loren Miller, a great friend and senior political science colleague, later admitted that "even though I may have not been all that accurate in my presentation, they really liked my energy and passion for the discipline. I had a presence that would command interest in the discipline."

Sure enough, about two days later, Helen DuPont of Human Resources tele-phoned and offered me the position. Though I still had two other on-campus in-terviews pending, I accepted the position—"a bird in the hand is better than two in the bush." Janet and I were ecstatic. In the summer of 1995, with the help of my brother Philip, we loaded a U-Haul and moved to North Texas.

In June of 1996, I completed my dissertation and earned my Ph.D. in Politi-cal Science. There were tears of joy. Who would have thought that a guy like me could have gone "all the way" in academia? It took me only nine years, and I did it! Due to the distance, I didn't attend the ceremony but I did indeed celebrate.

While at Collin County Community College, I became very active in the community. In 1997 one of my colleagues, History Professor Joe Jaynes, was running for local County Commissioner. He was seeking help and of course I would do anything to help a fellow colleague. Joe became County Commissioner in 1998. Ironically, it was also during this time that my Dad decided to run for City Council in St. Cloud, Florida. Though he got beat, I marveled at this man, who came to this county with nothing, pursuing the greatest role that our political system offers.

And then I met Judge John Payton. Judge Payton is a Justice of the Peace. His precinct covers the North Dallas suburbs, mainly the cities of Allen and Plano. But he was more than that. At that time, he was the youngest elected official in the history of the United States. In 1990, at 18 years old, he shocked the world when he beat a career incumbent. We immediately bonded and became friends.

John is very articulate, likeable, and knows how to interact with people. He has the type of personality that "you can't help but like the guy." Judge Payton is a true leader.

I had never been part of a legitimate Inner-Circle. Judge Payton would take me deep into the trenches of local politics. I began to watch his every move. Through his guidance, I met the major players in the community and party. I took mental and written notes. It was about this time that I became more involved and vocal with local and state politics.

Though I had knowledge of the political system, I was still raw in the leadership department. I decided to polish up on this shortcoming by being part of every organization that I could muster. From the Kiwanis Club to the Sons of the American Legion to the Texas State Rifle Association, I was learning the system. I was also making my move to eventually run for political office.

In early 1991, I met with Judge Payton at his house. We held a meeting about the state of our federal representation in D.C. over pizza and PlayStation. I wanted John to run against the lethargic incumbent Congressman, Sam Johnson. After hours of discussion, John refused because he felt the timing wasn't right. He had some personal issues to address such as completing his higher education.

So, I told John, "Hey, if you won't do it, then I will." John made it clear that as my friend he supports the decision, but as an elected official he can only do so much. I understood.

When I told Janet of my plans, though it would be a challenge, she supported my decision. At this time Janet was also pregnant with our son, Dante. Yet, I was so passionate about the state of our nation. I was willing to do whatever I needed to make our country better. I now had to organize a strategy to do what my friend John Payton had done earlier and "shock the world."

# District 3 and the Incumbent

After the 2000 census, the state of Texas had to redistrict. Because of its population boom, Texas was going to gain at least two new Congressional districts. In Texas, the state legislature has the primary responsibility for creating a redistricting plan, subject to approval by the state governor.

With the partisan Republican majority now in charge of redistricting, gerrymandering (the deliberate manipulation of political boundaries for electoral advantage, usually of incumbents or a specific political party) was at an all time high. As such, before an electoral strategy could be formulated, I had to study the territory that had to be conquered: Congressional District 3.

The Third District of Texas encompasses parts of Northern Dallas and Southern Collin counties including all or part of the cities of Murphy, Dallas, Frisco, Rowlett, Garland, Richardson, Melissa, McKinney, New Hope, Princeton, Lowry Crossing, Fairview, Lucas, Allen, Plano, Parker, St. Paul, Wylie, and Sachse.

The region is one of the fastest growing in the nation and is the corporate home of several Fortune 500 companies such as Cinemark Theatres, Frito Lay, Dr. Pepper, Electronic Data Systems (EDS), JC Penny, and Texas Instruments. The Third District boasts several nationally recognized public school districts and universities such as the University of Texas at Dallas (UTD) and the Collin County Community College District (CCCCD).

I wasn't sure where the new congressional districts were going to be created, but I knew that there was no way they would draw the incumbent Republican congressman out of his current residency in the city of Plano. There was speculation that Dallas, Garland, and Richardson were going to be placed in the new district. So, my plan was to focus mainly on the 230,000+ people who were living in Plano.

Plano is located mainly within Collin County, but also extends into Denton County. According to the 2005 census estimate, the city population was 250,096. Plano is within the Dallas/Plano/Irving metropolitan division of the Dallas/Fort Worth/Arlington metropolitan area; a title designated by the U.S. Census, and is colloquially referred to as the Dallas/Fort Worth Metroplex.

The population of the district is predominately white. There are some racial and ethnic minorities, such as Hispanics, African Americans, and Asians in the area. But, they either did not participate or aligned with the Democratic Party. For example, all of the county commissioners, city council members, state representatives and senators in District 3 are white.

Due to the aforementioned, I decided to run for political office as a Republican. Granted that I was very involved with the party at the grassroots level, I wasn't happy with the Republican party at the national level. Still, with the knowledge that the District and County voted over 80% Republican, I had no choice but to run as a Republican.

My next step was to visit the Collin County Elections Office. I wanted to view the data and see exactly what the voter turnout was in prior congressional elections. I had visited the location on many occasions for academic and personal reasons. Due to these stopovers, I made some contacts in the office. Sharon Rowe, the appointed Elections Administrator, knew of me and always treated me with professionalism.

Asking questions from an academic rather than candidate perspective, Sharon answered all my queries. I was sent to their updated website which had most of the information I needed online. I spent the next few days examining all the information.

The results were very intriguing. I examined the last five Republican primary election results. The numbers were shocking. I knew that voter turnout was bad, but the empirical data showed that less than 10% of the registered voters would vote in the Republican primary (the Democratic Party maybe garnered 1% of the vote). Though I was only looking at Collin County numbers, the Dallas County results were quite similar.

It was clear that this District was Republican turf. In most of these elections, the incumbent wasn't even opposed in the general election. Likewise, because the state of Texas has straight-party voting, some 75% of those who voted in the primary election voted Republican in the general election. These numbers proved that if I won the Republican primary, which is an open primary state, I would win the general election. (Collin County Elections Office, http://www.co.collin.tx.us/elections/election_results/1996/index.jsp)

I was seeking office in a non-presidential election year. Unlike 2000, the 1998 election data showed that an embarrassingly six percent turned out to vote in the Republican primary. I figured that the turnout in 2002 would be similar. To be safe, I estimated high with the number of 8,000 total votes to become the next congressman for District Three.

The District's incumbent congressman was and still is, Sam Johnson. Sam Johnson served in the U.S. Air Force for 29-years as a highly decorated pilot. He flew combat missions in both the Korean and Vietnam Wars. He was also a prisoner of war in Hanoi for nearly seven years. A decorated war hero, Johnson was awarded two Silver Stars, two Legions of Merit, the Distinguished Flying Cross, one Bronze Star with Valor, two Purple Hearts, four Air Medals, and three Outstanding Unit Awards.

After his military career, he established a home-building business and served in the Texas state legislature. He then ran and won his race for U.S. Congress in 1991.

With these credentials, I knew that a challenge to this "icon" would have to be sensitive and without rancor. I respect what Sam did for our country and value his service. I would have to make it clear to all that I wasn't running against Sam Johnson. Rather, I was running for the U.S. Congress. I thought and still believe that he is not an effective representative.

In my opinion, the incumbent is a slothful legislator. Sam Johnson sits on the powerful Ways and Means Committee, as well as the Education Committee. He hasn't done enough to directly help the District in either area. I am not recommending pork-barrel legislation. Rather, that he use his position to steer appropriate revenue to coincide with the growth in the District.

He also doesn't keep his promises. He broke his oath to the landmark *1994 Contract with America* as it pertains to specific term limits. Due to either age or incompetence, he had introduced and/or sponsored little if any legislation. His main themes and voting record exclusively focused on a strong national defense, the right to life, gun rights, and taxes.

At 70+ years old, I believed he lacked the energy and enthusiasm to effectively represent the District. From informal polls, and off the record comments, most folks agreed. But because of his POW status and past, the incumbent was endowed to be the District's congressman until he felt otherwise. I guess the logic here is that this was the "least" the community could do because of his and family's suffering. I now had to organize a strategy that would somehow overcome these formidable realities.

# Let's Get Ready To Run For Office

After weeks of contemplation and thought, I decided on my strategy. Though there is no political science definition, I called it "Operation Shock the World." The strategy placed emphasis on three central themes: 1) Quad-Voter Targeting; 2) Grassroots Campaigning; and, 3) Cross-Over Voting.

In basic campaigning, voter targeting deals with the candidate placing all the energy and resources trying to garner one group of voters. Conventional wisdom states that candidates should always target registered voters. I agree. If one wants the best odds at winning an election, one must target this cluster of voters. By looking at the voter's history, the best group for me to target was registered Republicans who voted in the 1996, 1998, and 2000 Republican primary.

Likewise, I decided to take voter targeting a step further. Since the District has experienced dramatic growth, I was determined to target voters who voted in the 2000 presidential election. Since over 70% of those who voted Republican in 2000 general election punched the "straight-party Republican" ticket, I was confident that most new Republicans didn't even know their congressman.

The third piece of voter targeting placed emphasis on the non-voter. Regardless of their party affiliation, I would go after every person in the District. Studies show that this approach is reckless, because these folks do not participate. When it comes to civic engagement and participation, they are apathetic and ignorant. To an extent, I agreed. But the numbers clearly stated that I needed less than 10,000 votes to be their next congressman. This was especially true with the hundreds of ostracized ethnic and racial minorities in the community. The same held true for the neglected college students, whom I knew for sure, would garner their support. Every vote would count.

Lastly, the fourth branch of my voter targeting strategy was to woo teachers. Since I was an educator, I felt that they would unequivocally vote for "one of their own." I would make sure that they knew I would improve education and help bring funds to the District. Also, my fellow community college colleagues would be courted. It doesn't take a brain surgeon to figure out that my victory would be a triumph for the college and every employee.

Additionally, the bulk of the campaign would be a grassroots movement. My campaign would be person-to-person and walking door-to-door. Since most people did not know who I was or what I stood for, I felt that this was the single most important thing I could do.

Lastly, I had to convince Democrats, Libertarians, and Independents to "cross-over" and vote for me. Though the Democrats were thinking about running their own candidate, I felt confident that I could convince them otherwise. The Libertarians were few, but again every vote would count.

I was confident that "Operation Shock the World" offered me the best opportunity to defeat the career incumbent. My chances were already slim to none, so it would have been ludicrous to settle on the traditional electoral methods and campaign strategies. It was crystal clear that this unconventional electoral strategy had no middle-ground. I would either upset the incumbent or get thumped by him like every other candidate.

Moreover, as a full-time Professor of Political Science at Collin County Community College (CCCC), I had to make sure that the President of the College approved and supported my decision. As long as it wasn't for a CCCC Board of Trustees position, my contract and faculty handbook allowed me to seek public office. I still respected President Israel and wanted him to be aware of my electoral effort.

I met with Dr. Cary Israel and we examined the pros and cons. Though he was limited to the role he could play in my campaign, he enthusiastically supported my decision as well as my right to run for elective office.

President Israel came to CCCC from Raritan Valley Community College (NJ) a few years earlier. Because of his commitment to educational excellence and appealing personality, we immediately bonded. The two of us would chat quite frequently. He became my mentor. Under his leadership, he transformed CCCC from a mediocre regional institution, into a national and international educational juggernaut.

I started to "leak" information that I was running for U.S. Congress. I formed an "Exploratory Committee," and started to get organized. I went to the Elections Office and picked up all the relevant forms and paperwork. I stopped by the party headquarters and dropped off some exploratory cards to draw some support. I couldn't believe the negative "look" that the party chairman, Buddy Ragley, gave me.

Buddy called me into his private office and suggested that I consider running for something else. He said, "You would be better off running for County Commissioner or the new State House seat." He garbled a few more condescending and unprofessional comments. I smiled and gave him a line to the extent that, "I am just in the exploratory stage, and not quite sure if I am going to run anyway."

As I headed home, to be honest, I started to rethink my campaign run. I knew that running for office was going to be demanding. Working full-time and campaigning was going to consume almost all my time. But the shabby treatment that I was already experiencing really bothered me. I was very surprised by how badly the Chairman had treated me. I knew it was wrong and unfair, but it was the reality of politics.

Then I thought: if the Chairman was so adamant against me running for office, maybe he was afraid that I could beat his "boy!" Deep down, maybe he knew that I could indeed win. As I pulled into my driveway, I vowed to not let his patronizing or any other person's negative comments deter me from my objective. I later told my Inner-Circle of the treatment and it equally motivated them to work harder.

In late-January of 2001, I decided to call a Saturday evening meeting to start the campaign process. My friend, Syrous Malek, offered his home for the event. It was at this time I presented "Operation Shock the World." In the months prior to this meeting, I conversed with many friends and people whom I trusted. I invited them to this meeting.

During my high-tech presentation, I labeled them as "Leaders" in my "Inner-Circle." I created a name for this committee, "Caiazzo for Congress." I explained that I trusted each of them, and that they would know things about the campaign that no one else would know. Besides Dr. Malek, there were about fifteen people in attendance. I vividly remember Mary Matusik, Mark Hultgren, Jon Hewitt, Tiam Tavokoli, and Daryl Irland.

I had some other close friends who wanted to be part of my Inner-Circle, but I didn't feel comfortable putting them in these leadership positions. See, if I didn't listen to the advice or comments from these close friends, I am sure their feelings would be hurt. So, I was very selective with my Inner-Circle.

I wanted people who believed in my cause and were willing to diligently work to achieve victory. I wasn't interested in keeping everyone happy. I was running to win.

Throughout the meeting I was challenged and asked questions. I promised them that when I won, they would all serve with me either in D.C. or in the District. I guaranteed them that I would give 110%. I stressed that if we won, they would also all be recognized as some of the greatest political consultants in America. Because if we pulled this off, everyone in academia and in the political world would want to know the "who, what, when, where, and how" of our campaign. I reaffirmed that this unorthodox strategy would either make or break us. In short, I stated that: "we would either pull off the greatest campaign victory in the history of congressional politics, or get a mud-hole stomped on us and stomped dry!" They all agreed to volunteer and help me in this endeavor.

As the days went on, I had to select a campaign treasurer. Election laws mandated that I have one. The selection of a campaign manager is very important since this person's name will be on everything that had to do with the campaign. They will be the custodian of the finances and responsible for keeping track of all revenue.

Since I was serving as the candidate and campaign manager, there was no way to use myself. Likewise, since Janet was pregnant, placing her in a stressful leadership position was out of the question. I decided to ask my good friend, Mary Matusik.

In my opinion, Mary was the perfect person for the position. She is very intelligent, active in the community, and very well organized. She is attractive, has an engaging personality, and is incredibly energetic. Most importantly, she was disgruntled with the incumbent and represented the characteristics of population that I was trying to woo. She believed in me and accepted the position without reservations.

Mary and I became educated on the election laws and the rules put forth by the Federal Election Commission (FEC). Though I hadn't officially announced my candidacy, nor did we know exactly what District I would be running in, we got every thing organized and filled out. We just waited for all to be set.

We also had to figure out and set a budget. It should be noted that the average cost of a congressional campaign in 2002 was roughly two to three million dollars. Some candidates would raise and spend more. I didn't think we needed to raise and spend more than $15,000. Yes, only $15,000! I have always argued that one's vote is more important than their money. I believed that by running a grassroots campaign like ours, money wouldn't be all that important.

My Inner-Circle and I decided to write out our campaign platform. We opted to select four to five issues that would be the central theme of the campaign. We emphasized the following planks: 1) A Strong National Defense; 2) Improving Public Education; 3) Lowering Taxes and Tax Relief for Small Businesses; 4) Federal Scholarships and Book Stipends for Higher Education; and, 5) All Federal Road Construction Projects will be done at night.

Basic campaign school 101 states that candidates should target the most important issues that concern the majority of voters. I spiced in this logic by adding issues that I personally believed in. I am passionate about improving higher education. I believe then and even now, that the state and federal government isn't doing enough to assist and reform higher education.

My next objective was to put together my literature. I decided that when my team and I went door knocking, I should have an introductory piece of literature to hand to people once they answer the door. Since everything was still in limbo, I ordered these materials from a company on the internet. I called them "Greeting Cards."

My good friend, Chuck Lalanne, took a picture of me with a digital camera. I sent it to the company as an attachment. They put my picture on the front of the card along with some basic information. The cards were printed on both sides, and about one-third the size of a normal 8 ½ by 11-inch piece of paper. Because of wear and tear, I had them printed on sixty pound card stock.

I ordered 500 cards. I had the company make another 250 "door-hangers" with the same information. These door-hangers would have a slit on the top of the card. If someone wasn't home, I would just leave them my greeting card on their doorknob.

I decided that it was time to dress and look congressional. I got a haircut that was more conservative. I purchased a few new suits for the campaign. I traded in my blue jeans and knit shirts, for Polo pants and oxford shirts and ties. I was going to dress for success.

It should be noted that one just can't run for political office. You have to meet each state's ballot access requirements. To run for U.S. Congress in Texas, one would either pay a $1,500 filing fee or collect 500 signatures of registered voters. I opted to do the latter.

With the help of many supporters, I attained more than the required 500 signatures. I actually collected 510 signatures on my own. However, when verified, many of those signatures were thrown out. They were either not registered to vote, had an expired registration card, didn't live in the District, or gave me improper information.

I knew this was probable so others helped me garner signatures. I was ever so thankful to the following people that collected signatures: Miguel Alarcon (a Democrat); Angelo D'Salvo (a WWII veteran); Dean Hull (former student); Daryl and Jennie Irland; Sheila Burkhalter (friend); Zonk; Mary Matusik; Josh Andor (former student and member of the local Princeton School Board); Jasmina Fahrendorff (friend); and, Tiam Tavokoli (student).

I decided to purchase the list of registered voters in the District. Daryl Ireland and I went to the Election's Office and purchased the CD. This CD cost roughly $100. It had all the voter information that we requested broken down by name, address, phone number, etc. We spent hours at his parent's home printing off pages and pages of this data. We looked at the District map and organized by street the houses we would visit door-to-door. And Daryl was only 21 years old.

Daryl Irland was a student in my American Government class back in 2000. He took my class his first semester in college. Even though he was very articulate, I would often have to emphasize the course rules and rancor policy during class discussions. I valued his input and we became friends when the semester concluded. I saw lots of potential in Daryl and took him under my wing as a younger brother, per se. I saw a lot of me in him.

Daryl wouldn't let me down. After the campaign and completion of his two-year degree at CCCC, he transferred to DePaul University in Chicago (IL). He enrolled in the Marketing Program and recently graduated with his Bachelors degree. At present, he has a great career and is still living in the Chicago area.

As March of 2001 approached, it seemed obvious that Congressional District 3 wouldn't change much. I met with my Inner-Circle and we discussed the possibility of announcing early. Others thought that if I announced too early, then the incumbent would be better prepared. A few suggested that I wait for the last minute.

I thought announcing early was a good idea. It would get me early name recognition and hopefully drum up some support. Rumor had it that the incumbent's health wasn't all that great, and that he may not even run for re-election. Deep down, I was hoping that a tough campaign would force the career incumbent to retire.

After much deliberation, I chose to announce early. Though the lines for District 3 weren't finalized, I completed all the paperwork to run for the U.S. Congress as a Republican. Since state party law wouldn't allow me to put "Dr." or "Ph.D." on the application and ballot, I opted to use Thomas "Tom" Caiazzo. Surprisingly, I received little press coverage.

# Fundraising

If there is one thing that irritates me more than anything, it is when a political candidate asks me for money. Ironically, I now had to ask people for money to run for office. This really bothered me. I know that it takes money to run a campaign. I wasn't affluent, so I couldn't self-finance my campaign. I would have to approach my family, friends, and others and ask them for donations. And I needed to raise at least $15,000. Since this was the reality, I decided to set some parameters.

First, I wouldn't accept any money without giving something in return. No matter what, be it a hot dog or a t-shirt, people would get something in return for a donation. Second, I wouldn't take any donation over $1,000. I didn't think this would be a problem, but just in case.

Lastly, I would not accept any political action committee (PAC) money. PACs are committees formed by business, labor, or other special-interest groups to raise money and make contributions to the campaigns of political candidates whom they support. Federal PACs are limited in the amount of money that they can contribute to other organizations, at most $5,000 per candidate per election. Elections such as primaries, general elections and special elections are counted separately: a) $15,000 per political party per year, and, b) $5,000 per PAC per year. However, PACs are not limited to advertising spent on the support of their own issues.

We really didn't have a fundraiser committee, but Daryl's mother, Jennie Irland, took the leadership role. We vowed to never charge people anything at our fundraisers, but to only accept donations. Jennie, as well as most people in the campaign, is a great cook. So, I knew that no matter what food activity we did, it would be a success.

At that time, federal law mandated that an individual can only give a candidate seeking federal office $1,000 per election year (it is now $2,000). Thus, the first people I approached for money were my family. Besides the $1,000 that Janet and I put from our personal savings, I went to my parents. They contributed $1,000. Likewise, my brothers contributed another $1,000.

I decided to tap into my connections and try to organize some "high profile" speakers for fundraisers. I would ask sports entertainers and professional athletes that I knew through someone or knew personally. For their time, I would pay their transportation, meals, lodging, etc. In return, I could raise money at a dinner or rally.

The first contact I approached was professional boxer and former champion of the world, Larry Holmes. I met Larry through my cousin Ralph in the Lehigh Valley, Pennsylvania. I called and made all arrangements. After arriving at the Allentown/Bethlehem/Easton (ABE) airport, Ralph picked me up and we immediately went to Larry's restaurant in Easton (PA).

It was nice to see Larry. We had lunch and I explained to him my situation. My goal was to bring in high profile athletes and entertainers to both help me raise money and draw support. Larry liked the idea. Due to Larry's busy schedule, I had to speak to his agent regarding all the particulars. I thanked Larry.

His agent was very professional. We organized some dates and times. His agent asked about money, and I again reminded him that my goal was for civic empowerment and Larry could help me ignite and rally new voters. I would cover Larry's fees and other related expenses. We concluded our meeting on a positive note, and I was to call back when I returned to Texas.

Unfortunately, Larry's agent and I couldn't come to an agreement. The bottom-line was that the agent wanted his client to receive a fee for his appearance. I am not sure if the fee was really for Larry or the agent. After calculating the cost of the dinner, advertising, Larry's fee, and other related expenses, I opted to cancel this fundraiser. I would have lost money.

Over the next few months, I diligently tried to secure other "high-profile" personalities. Though many claimed to be very supportive of my electoral pursuit and wanted to help empower the electorate, they still wanted to be compensated for their effort. From the start, I never had a problem with paying these men and women for the basic particulars. However, some of their fees were ludicrous.

For example, I contacted the agent for the legendary Pete Rose. In fact, I met the agent and Pete a few months earlier at a sports memorabilia show in Plano (TX). I was told that Pete would say a few words on my behalf, discuss the importance of voting, sign a few autographs and hats for two hours (no bats or gloves), for roughly $10,000!

With some connections in the professional wrestling industry, I contacted the World Wrestling Entertainment (WWE). Since wrestling is very popular, especially with young people, as well as the company promoting a major voter registration drive (SMACKDOWN the VOTE), I thought this would be a great opportunity to garner support and raise money.

When I attained the price list of these wrestlers, I was shocked. I was advised that the price for professional wrestling legend Undertaker's service was $20,000. Two other icons of the sports entertainment industry, Hulk Hogan, and Ric Flair didn't return my calls and e-mails. I got "body-slammed" with that approach.

The only personality that I received a "fair" offer came from a service in Dallas that handled the appearances of Dallas Cowboy football players. Since the Asian community had grown so quickly in the District, I thought the $2,500 asking price for Cowboy linebacker, Dat Nguyen, was a fair price. Dat was the first Vietnamese American to play in the National Football League. Unfortunately, I couldn't secure a venue to hold the fundraiser in a cost-effective manner.

I tried to generate support from some music groups with Dallas' ties. I was equally stunned by the prices of some groups such as the Toadies and Hootie and the Blowfish. Some didn't even return my e-mails and/or phone calls. One group, FrogNot, was very positive but for some reason things didn't work out.

My "high-profile" ambitions were quickly evaporated. Call it idealism or being naïve, I thought that some of these folks would volunteer their time and effort for civic engagement. I was categorically wrong. It was all about money.

Nonetheless, with a start up base of $5,000, I felt that was plenty of revenue to purchase the campaign basics – literature, name-tags, signs, shirts, etc. With that money, Jon Hewitt ordered 500 t-shirts for $1,000. The t-shirts were white, with "It Begins With You in 2002," printed in blue and red, with an elephant and the "Caiazzo for Congress" on the front.

I went to a local shirt store and purchased fifteen, polo-collar shirts for my Inner-Circle. They were navy blue, with the "Caiazzo for Congress" emblem embroidered above the pocket. These shirts were very professional but could also be worn in a casual setting. They cost me $15 each.

I purchased my first set of campaign signs. I purchased 200 yard signs. They had a white background with blue lettering. It read: "Caiazzo for Congress." It had the district, date, and disclaimer on the bottom. I ordered them from a local business, Cartwright Signs, and the bill was roughly $500. I went to Home Depot and purchased the nails and stakes. Miguel Alacarn, Rick Nolan, Zonk, Jon Hewitt, Jerry Mahan, Daryl Irland, and a few others nailed them together in Miguel's garage one Saturday afternoon.

The first fundraiser was at my friend Marty Berryman's house. Marty and his wife Sharon opened their home in the country for my "Kickoff." It was a huge BBQ and we invited everyone that we could think of. Since it was in June of 2001, the weather was quite toasty. But we had enough beverages and food to keep everyone satisfied. Chuck Lalanne even arranged for a live band.

About 300 people showed-up. It was a diverse gathering, including members from my Kiwanis Club, students and staff from the college, and, friends in the community. I was very pleased. I was there early and greeted one and all. I walked around and talked to everyone as they were eating. I was literally shaking hands and kissing babies.

We ate brisket, hamburgers, baked beans, and corn. We drank soda, water, and beer from a keg. I gave away t-shirts and signed people up to help in the campaign. It was very energetic and people were excited about the campaign.

Throughout all my fundraisers, I never ate anything until after the event was over. Not to offend, I would never sit at anyone's table. I would touch people on their shoulders and hug when appropriate. Not only was this my nature, but it would also show people that I really cared for them.

About half-way through the event, Marty introduced me to the audience. With a pregnant Janet by my side, I gave a short but enthusiastic speech about how this campaign is about change. I said, "This campaign is about energy and new blood. It was about someone who will represent all the people, not just the special interests. The experts say I don't have a chance. But with your support, together we will prove them wrong. Together we will take back OUR House and bring forth new leadership. It Begins with You in 2002."

When the Kickoff ended, everyone was exhausted. It was a long day and I was very eager to read the final Volunteer list. There were over 30 names. This was great. Mary pulled me to the side and said, "Do you want to know how much money we raised?" I was more excited about the sign-up list, but said, "Sure!" There was close to $300 in the jar. Not bad.

I promised Marty and Sharon that I and a few others would return in the morning to clean-up. I again thanked them for their hospitality. Judge Payton and I conversed after the event. He was impressed with the turnout and gave me some suggestions for future events. I went home feeling very satisfied.

The next morning produced one of the funniest moments of the campaign. All of my fundraisers produced lasting memories. Some were good and some were bad. But many were funny. For example, as I drove up to Marty's house to clean up last evening's mess, I see about four people already there: Chuck Lalanne and his two sons, Zack and Jacob; Daryl Irland; and, Aimee Johnson. They pretty much had everything cleaned-up.

The only thing left was the keg of beer. I had to bring the keg back by 12:00 noon. Chuck and Marty, not wanting to waste the beer, decided to drink as much of it as they could. We were all busting at the seams as Marty and Chuck are frantically searching the entire house for jugs and glasses to store the beer for later consumption. When I loaded the now empty keg on my truck, both of my friends were blitzed—and it was probably only 11:00am!

Along with the entire Inner-Circle, Jennie decided that we should organize our fundraiser schedule. We scrolled through the calendar and decided on the "what's and where's" of our fundraisers. We eventually settled on doing four more fundraisers: in September, a "Labor Day" weekend pool party at my house; a "BBQ and Yard Sale" at Mary's house in late October; an "Italian Dinner and Silent Auction" at the American Legion Hall in November; and, an early January "Dinner with Tom" at Jennie's house. Combined, we thought that these events could both raise money and garner support.

The "Labor Day" weekend pool party was very successful in the terms of turnout. About 100 people showed up. My neighbor and friend Jerry Mahan, along with my Inner-Circle, helped me with the set-up. We had lots of food and garnered many more volunteers. My good friend John Binder volunteered his band, Dos Hombres, for the day. Sorry to say, at the end of the evening, there was only about $100 in the jar. The "BBQ and Yard Sale" at Mary's house produced almost identical results. I was disappointed.

The next two scheduled fundraisers did much better from the fiscal standpoint. The "Italian Dinner and Silent Auction" did very well because all of the items were donated. We had clothing, jewelry, sports tickets, pottery, etc. It was a decent evening. We raised about $300.

At this event, Angelo was asked to lead the Pledge of Allegiance and introduce me. Angelo DiSalvo, 83 years old and a WWII war hero, is a great man. He also thinks he is a comedian. After the Pledge, Angelo decided to tell a few jokes. It was fine until one of his jokes was slightly "off-color." I cringed as Greg and Mary Dennis ogled me as their 8 and 10 year old sons were unnecessarily subjected to the profanity. I would make it up to the Dennis' family later in the evening, when I asked their youngest son at the time, Fielder, to cut the cake. To this day, Greg and I banter about the "Angelo" incident.

I also remember three elected officials in attendance: Josh Andor (Princeton School Board Member); Judge John Payton (Justice of the Peace); and, Judge Tom Kelly (Justice of the Peace). Toward the end of the event, Judge Kelly gave me some information that reenergized me. As a Vietnam veteran, Judge Kelly stated that the incumbent had done little to help Veterans in the District. The Veterans at the local VA hospital didn't even have "adequate socks, underwear, or hygiene products." He continued by implying that Sam uses his POW status "to get re-elected."

I needed to hear these candid comments, especially from a entrenched party loyalist and popular elected official. I respect Judge Kelly and have always supported his campaign. He is a great person and has done a lot for the community. I was also angry because our Veterans deserve better. Deep down, I now considered the incumbent a "POW pimp!" Unfortunately, when I contacted the media about the poor conditions at the local Veteran's hospital, I didn't even get a return call.

In early January of 2002 Richard Bingham, a friend and Elvis impersonator put on a professional wrestling fundraiser for my campaign in Princeton (TX). Though he didn't raise any money, he did get about sixty people to register to vote. It was a fun event, and I met many people, especially those who were discontent. I also watched Jeremy Young, Blake Wiggins, Lvis, Bigfoot, Cowboy Easy E, and other local wrestling talents put on a decent wrestling show.

The Tavakoli family was very supportive with my political campaign. They owned a pizza restaurant in central Plano, "Little T's." Their daughter, Tiam, was part of my Inner-Circle and we often used her parent's place to meet. On many occasions, Mohsen and Fatemeh Tavakoli let us use their establishment for voter registration drives. They often donated food as well.

In the end, after all the fundraisers, donations, in-kind contributions and all other collections, I raised approximately $13,282, with $12,282 (92.5%) coming from individual contributions. Though we were short some $2000 of our projections, the committee felt we could make up the fiscal limitation with additional door-knocking and hard-work. In contrast, the incumbent raised nearly $1 million, with approximately $428,625 (48.7%) coming from PAC contributions. He received one-hundred and nineteen $1,000 checks compared to my six.

I would later be part of the Plaintiffs' Fact Witness Testimony in the landmark case, McConnell v. FEC i.e. "McCain-Feingold Bill. This Bipartisan Campaign Reform Act of 2002 (BCRA) is U.S. Congressional legislation which regulates the financing of political campaigns. Named after its chief sponsors, Senators John McCain (AZ, R) and Russ Feingold (WS, D), the law became effective on 6 November 2002. The new legal limits became effective on 1 January 2003.

As noted in a Supreme Court ruling on the BCRA, it was designed to address three issues: 1) the increased role of soft money in campaign financing; 2) the proliferation of issue ads; and, 3) what were regarded as disturbing campaign practices during the federal elections of 1996, including (to some degree) the presidential race.

The BCRA produced some interesting results, some which I agree and others that I disagree. Here are the major provisions: 1) a wholesale prohibition on soft money contributions and expenditure to national political parties—unlimited donations nominally made for non-campaign purposes, but potentially used to influence federal elections; 2) a prohibition on soft money contributions and expenditure to state and local political parties, with a few limited exceptions; 3) Federal candidates and officeholders prohibited from accepting or spending soft money; 4) a ban on supposedly non-partisan "issue ads" funded by soft money from corporations and labor unions—those referring to candidates for federal election without expressly advocating their election or defeat—in the 60 days prior to a general election, or 30 days prior to a primary election; 5) disclosure of sources of finance for "electioneering communications" in excess of $10,000 per year; 6) a political party spending money in a general election campaign must choose between making coordinated expenditures on behalf of its candidate, or independent expenditures on behalf of its candidate, but not both. (Ruled unconstitutional in McConnell v. FEC, but later upheld by the Supreme Court); 7) minors are prohibited from making contributions to candidates and political parties. (ruled unconstitutional by the Supreme Court); 8) hard money legal limits raised: a) limit for individual contributions per candidate per election increased from $1,000 to $2,000; b) limit for individual contributions to National Party Committees increased from $20,000 to $25,000 per year; and, c) limit for individual contributions to state and local party committees increased from $5,000 to $10,000. Other provisions (incomplete); and, 8) Fundraising on federal property is prohibited.

# Party Politics

From the start, the local Republican Party was against me running for U.S. Congress. The main person behind this fact was the Collin County Republican party chairman, Buddy Ragdley. A party loyalist for years, he operated in a manner very similar to the old party machines of the 1960s with Richard Daly and even earlier with Tammany Hall that controlled New York city politics.

By the nature of the position, Mr. Ragdley had a tremendous influence over the county and district politicians. More importantly, he was very involved with the precinct chairs and other supporters. There were also other off-shoot Republican organizations that he had influence over such as the: Republican Men's Club, Young Republicans, and the Golden Corridor Republican Women's Club. With this said, it was clear from the outset that the local Republican Party Chairman, and thus the other organizations, did not want me or anybody running against Sam Johnson.

One of the basic fundamental purposes of a political party is to sponsor candidates for office. In a primary election, the Chairman and party are not supposed to take sides or support a candidate. Once the primary produces a winner, the party should then do all it can to secure victory for their candidate. In my case, the Chairman covertly and overtly supported the career incumbent.

After announcing an exploratory campaign for U.S. Congress, I started to receive "dirty-looks" and felt very uncomfortable at Republican Party events. People, some who I thought I knew well, would go out of their way not to talk or sit near me. I confided in some people about the problem, and it was made clear that many folks in the party didn't want me running against the incumbent. The Chairman was the main player behind the dissatisfaction.

At the time, I was the Advisor of the Collin County Community College (CCCCR) College Republicans. The Chairman made allegations to the Club President that I was using them for my own advantage. The Chairman even had the audacity to contact my place of employment regarding the situation. The Club did indeed support my candidacy but did nothing improper or unethical. They supported me as individuals and not as a Club.

Even when the local Republican Party sponsored candidate events, they were put on in a way to set me up for failure. It was clear by the questions asked, that they were supportive of the incumbent. By the way, the party and every organization in the community refused my request to sponsor a debate. Why? He insulted the community by often saying he didn't have the "time." I know he was scared to death to debate me. I would have "cleaned his clock." In fact, the incumbent only showed up to one joint event and that was a simple three minute presentation. I wasn't even treated as a legitimate candidate.

At one Republican Party candidate "meet and greet" forum, I gave a brief, time allotted three-minute presentation. The audience could then ask questions. Out of all the other candidates from a variety of local and state offices (by the way, my incumbent opponent was "too busy" working to attend), I was asked the most questions. And they weren't fluffy or supportive. Some included questions about: my prior membership in the ACLU and Sierra Club; what I thought about electronic voting; and, abortion and gay rights. I answered candidly and truthfully. I sensed the packed crowd didn't like my answers, but if I wooed one person, my mission was accomplished.

My campaign treasurer, Mary Matusik, also received some insulting jargon. Mary called me one day and said that she ran into one of Sam's campaign workers at the grocery store. He told Mary that my campaign was "political suicide." She also received an arrogant phone call from the incumbent's campaign director, Clark Briner. He never had the backbone to call me directly.

Clark Briner is a professional political consultant and member of the career incumbent's staff. He resides in Dallas and gets compensated quite well for his services. During my campaign period alone, official federal expenditure statements show that Clark received approximately a whopping $130,000 for his services for the one election cycle. This includes a $3,689 Christmas bonus in November of 2002. His Christmas bonus was 25% of my entire campaign budget!

My committee and other supporters even witnessed this discrimination. But you know what? I didn't quit. Neither did my committee. In fact, it made us work harder. It also proved that I was a viable candidate and the incumbent and his flunkies were concerned. Combine that with the fact that I knew I wasn't going to get the party loyalist vote anyway, I felt pretty good. And since I wouldn't quit, the party got nervous.

The Chairman and some of the party elders knew that Judge John Payton and I were friends. I guess this is why John was assigned to deliver me an urgent message. John told me that Richard Dotson wanted to have breakfast with the three of us. I asked "why," but John didn't know. I told John, "fine" and he arranged everything. He asked me to keep everything secret and not tell anyone. I only told Janet.

On a rainy winter Friday morning, John and I arrived in separate vehicles around 6:30am at a breakfast restaurant in Plano. Richard was already there and we shook hands and exchanged small talk. Richard Dotson is a major player with the Collin County Republican Party. He is very active in fundraising and helps organize their annual golf benefit.

He began to go into how I had great credentials and how I was going to be a major player for the party in the future, but for now, I needed to reconsider running against Sam Johnson.

As Richard was talking and giving me these back-handed compliments, I began getting annoyed. What arrogance to patronize me? I could sense that John knew nothing in advance about the meeting. He also seemed somewhat uncomfortable. Richard then made me an "offer he thought I couldn't refuse."

He said, "If you don't run for U.S. Congress BUT run for State Representative, I will make sure you have all the funding and support that you need to win." I looked at John. We were both stunned. Richard added a few additional comments. We concluded our breakfast meeting and I was told to get back with him in a few days regarding the offer.

As I headed to campus, I immediately called John from my cell phone. We spoke for some time and couldn't figure out if the offer was legitimate or realistic. I was angry that Mr. Dotson would even try to "buy" me, but John convinced me to take it as a compliment.

I thought about Richard's offer all weekend. At first, the offer looked quite appealing. I wouldn't have to worry about fundraising and at least some in the party would be supportive. On the other hand, I really liked the incumbent State Representative, Brian McCall, who he wanted me to run against. I also liked, even more, the person who was thinking about running against Mr. McCall, Fred Moses. Fred and his family were very supportive of my campaign. How could I break this allegiance? There was also no guarantee that I could or would win.

It should be noted that after I lost the election, Brian McCall sent me a handwritten letter complimenting me on my campaign effort. I was touched by the class act.

As a loyal person, I didn't want to let down all the people who have been helping me run for Congress. And maybe more importantly than anything, I wanted to run for U.S. Congress. I had an unprecedented strategy in place, and if successful, would revitalize the entire political system. This vision, more than anything else, led to my decision to turn-down Mr. Dotson's offer. I guess I cared more about the state of our system and nation, rather than my own selfish interests. How idealistic, huh?

As the weeks and months went on, I told some in my Inner-Circle about the offer. I think some were shocked that I didn't take the offer. Yet, it showed my loyalty to them and my commitment to our cause. After my loss to the incumbent in the primary, not one person in my Inner-Circle asked me if, in hindsight, I changed my mind about not taking Richard Dotson's offer. I worked too hard for them to think otherwise. Even though I lost, I took the high road.

I befriended another Republican candidate for public office, Andy Wollard. Andy is a family man and overall great guy. He is full of energy and has a passion for his community. Andy was running for a Justice of the Peace position in the precinct that represents the northwest part of the county (mainly the cities of Frisco, Celina, and Prosper). Andy is also treated unfairly by the local Republican party. Andy lost in both the 2002 and 2006 Republican primaries.

I am forever grateful to Andy because of an event that occurred one December evening during the campaign. Around 9:00pm on a chilly Friday night, I was putting out campaign signs along the busy interstate. Due to traffic, I tried to get my truck far enough away from the road, but not to close to the muddy ditch. Well, as I put out my final sign, I got stuck in the mud. I called AAA and telephoned Janet to advise it may be a long night. After talking to Janet, who was due in about three weeks, my cell phone battery died. Without my charger, I waited more than hour until a car pulled up behind me. It was Andy.

I was grateful to see Andy. He let me borrow his cell phone to both follow-up with AAA and to, more importantly, check on my expecting wife. I sat with Andy for about another hour until the wrecker pulled me out. Thank you, Andy!

Moreover, it was time to court the Democratic Party. Though I estimated that roughly two-thousand Democrats would vote in the 2002 primary, I was convinced that their support was needed to win. Following the cross-over voting strategy, I had to woo Democrats to cross-over in the primary and vote for me.

In a clandestine manner, I contacted the Collin County Democratic Party Chairman and invited him to dinner at the Austin Avenue cafe. He was very cordial and professional. I really liked his energy and personality. I explained to him my strategy. He appreciated the candor but had some concerns. First, he stated that "We plan to run a candidate for Congress." I said, "No problem. Since he will be unopposed, I just need for Democrats to vote for me in the primary."

Second, he wasn't quite sure that the party leaders would endorse such an idea. I understood, but tried to convince him that if I won, at least they would have access. The Democratic party would finally have a person who would listen to their needs. If victorious, I would even hire some Democrats to positions of leadership to show bipartisan support. I made it clear that his Democratic candidate didn't have a chance (I sensed he knew this), and I was the party's only hope for a voice.

We parted and he vowed to speak with the leadership and get back with me as soon as possible. Unfortunately, I had to get back with him. He told me that the leaders of the party would not endorse the cross-over voting strategy. I struck out with the Democrats.

In 2002, like I predicted, their candidate attained barely 20% of the vote in the general election. The party and their supporters still have no access or voice at the Congressional level or at any level of Collin County politics. It still bothers me that they didn't accept my offer.

I did the same cross-over approach with the local Libertarian party. Libertarians believe that you have the right to live your life as you wish, without the government interfering, as long as you don't violate the rights of others. Politically, this means Libertarians favor rolling back the size and cost of government, and eliminating laws that stifle the economy and control people's personal choices. I agree with many of their planks and had no concern about seeking their support.

I met with a group of Libertarians at Andy Piziali's home. Andy was the unofficial leader of the Libertarian Party in the region. We had a nice dinner and great conversation. I gave the same exact presentation that I gave to the Democrats. They were all very receptive and I am confident that they all worked hard to help me get elected. Unfortunately, they were very few in numbers; maybe less than fifty. So much for the cross-over voting strategy.

# The Bias and Hollow Media

Broadcast and print media play a major role in elections. From radio stations to television networks to newspapers, each vehicle should provide people with information on the candidates and their stance on the issues. Unfortunately, the media did an inadequate job with my congressional race.

It should be noted that the media's number one objective is to make a profit. It is true that they want to educate and inform the public, but everything the media does is advertisement driven. This is true for the national networks like FOX and CNN to the local affiliates.

With respect to my race for District 3, the major television networks didn't do anything with my campaign. The same for local radio. Only the local newspapers gave me coverage, and it was watershed at best. My campaign's website, www.tom2002.org, was probably my best vehicle to transmit information to the people.

The assumption going into the campaign was that my candidacy would draw a tremendous amount of media coverage. This stems from the fact that first and foremost I was running for the highest office in the District. Likewise, I was a political science professor and outsider challenging a career incumbent. It would make great press and produce a lot of coverage for the race. As one political consultant put it, "it would be like David taking on Goliath."

Since I announced my candidacy early, I was expecting a lot of media coverage. I worked with my press secretary, Champ Teng, to be prepared to debate, question, and challenge the incumbent on the issues. Champ joined my Inner-Circle near the middle of the campaign, and I wish he would have been there from the start. Still, to our chagrin, radio and television had no interest in the campaign. Though Champ did a great job with helping me campaign, little could be done to draw massive media coverage.

Champ Teng, who is currently the Chairman of the Board and CEO for Asian Beat News, Inc. was my press secretary. Champ was born in Cambodia and has served as President of the Cambodian-American Foundation in Washington D.C., where he played an important and critical role in helping to build better relations between the Cambodian people on both continents, as well as to establish contact with the governments of the United States and Cambodia.

It is implied that living in a large community, some of the radio and television networks would have at least interviewed me. They didn't. However, the incumbent would get coverage for his legislative activity in Washington. This was very prevalent after 9/11, when the former POW was on radio and TV what seemed like every day. I was never contacted. We asked for reciprocity. I'm still waiting.

I did use cable television to promote my campaign. Since I was on a limited budget, regular television was out of the question. The rates for commercial time on television networks varied. Though my one commercial ran on stations like CNN and FOX, they were limited.

The major cost of television advertising is not the commercial "rate," but the production of the commercial. You can't just use a basic camcorder. Commercial equipment and tapes are necessary. My one commercial cost roughly $300 to film and produce.

I also purchased time on the radio. Following the strategy, I thought the best station in the area to reach new voters was local ESPN talk radio frequency. For my radio spot, I had Texas Ranger super-fan and hometown icon, John J. "Zonk" Lanzillo, Jr., cut a radio ad with me asking sports fans for their support. It was a great ad and Zonk did a wonderful job. It cost more or less $500.

Though it wasn't major radio, I did manage to attain two local radio interviews. One was with a local Persian radio network and the other with a local Asian Indian frequency. Both radio personalities were very cordial and appreciative of my concern for their people.

Press releases were issued to all the major media outlets for all my appearances and functions. Some were printed. Most were not. The major paper of the District, the Dallas Morning News, gave me the basic coverage. Though the paper never interviewed me, they still endorsed the incumbent. After reading the paper's endorsement of the incumbent, I contacted the editorial board of the Dallas Morning News. I wanted to know their methodology and reasoning. I also wanted to know why they didn't contact me.

I was told that they sent me a questionnaire and invited me to their editorial office for an interview. After convincing them that there could have been a glitch because I got neither, I was curious as to why they didn't call or e-mail me. One would think that if I somehow didn't get the questionnaire, it would still be vital to contact me. The person said, "We don't contact candidates for endorsement via phone."

Since the congressional race would affect national decisions, the campaign even contacted national networks such as FOX and CNN. Information was sent to Rush Limbaugh and Bill O'Reilly. Articles and essays were sent to TIME, Newsweek, and the U.S. News and World Report. I received nothing from anyone. The only return received with a semi-generic reply was from Richard Benedetto of the USA TODAY.

I fared slightly better at the local level. The Plano Star Courier (PSC) newspaper gave me some coverage. The PSC is part of the Star Community Newspapers. These papers are a community newspaper group which serves the North Texas market, including three of the five fastest growing counties in Texas, as well as, three of the top twenty two fastest growing counties in the United States (Collin and Denton and Rockwall Counties). Star Community Newspapers publishes daily and weekly newspapers with meaningful editorial content covering local community news and events. Their total weekly circulation is approximately 200,000 households.

Prior to the campaign, I used to regularly write op-ed opinion pieces for the paper and its sister papers such as the Allen American and The McKinney Courier-Gazette. My students used to regularly write letters to their editors, so I had formed some favorable alliances and networks with them.

Despite the aforementioned, I was politically astute to know that a news reporter wasn't going to portray me in a positive manner. The few times I was interviewed, they were searching for things such as "why" I was running against the incumbent. They would print my planks, but they would never challenge the incumbent. For example, the incumbent swore to invoke term limits. When I stated in the paper that he violated his oath, the paper gave him a pass with his extraneous response: "the people can vote on term limits every two years."

It was equally shocking that not one organization in the entire District organized a debate. I continuously pointed this out to the press. In one article about a month before the election, Sam Johnson responded to my desire for a debate by stating that "he was too busy and had a lot of work to do." What arrogance! But what was equally depressing is that the paper let him get away with that statement! They did a pathetic job in challenging the incumbent on his record and stance on the issues.

Because of the bias and limited media coverage, I teetered with becoming more aggressive. My friend and colleague, Professor Oliver Jones, suggested that I openly challenge Sam Johnson to a debate- wearing a chicken outfit. Others suggested that I take off the "gloves" and call the incumbent out on his inept and slothful representation. These antics could increase media coverage.

Though deep down I really wanted to do the aforementioned, I was also trying to be more magnanimous. I had to keep reminding myself that if the strategy worked, I would become the District's next U.S. Congressman. I wanted to be perceived as a serious candidate and do nothing to damage the integrity of the position.

I also had to remember who I was running against. Sam Johnson was an aging POW. If I did anything too aggressive, it would be perceived as me being insensitive and disrespectful. In hindsight, I should have been more antagonistic and insistent.

In the end, the media is supposed to make people aware and informed. During the election season, they claim to cover the candidates and their issues. The local media in the region did a bias and terrible job with covering my campaign. There were no debates. I received no television or radio coverage. I wasn't even treated as a legitimate candidate.

# Grassroots Activities

The crux of the campaign's strategy was to garner electoral support via a grassroots campaign. Facing a career incumbent with a plethora of financial support, there was really no other campaign option. With less than 10% voting in past primary elections, my grassroots approach would mobilize new voters into the system. I would also hope to attain their support.

The term "grassroots" simply means a person to person campaign. In theory, if I would personally talk to one person and gain their support, then that person would tell someone else. And then that person would tell another. The trend would continue and spread, just like "grass."

With respect to this campaign strategy, my Inner-Circle was convinced that walking door-to-door was the single most important campaign tool to utilize. Since most people did not know me or my stance on the issues, door-knocking was the most practical approach.

We now had to consider when to start knocking door-to-door. A few people thought that eight months was too early and that people would forget by Election Day. Others advised that many voters don't focus on the election until a month or so before. Knowing the battle we faced, I stressed that though it may be too early and some may forget, there was a good possibility that I could pick up new campaign supporters and workers and we needed all the help we could get. We decided to start walking eight months before the election.

We also decided that we would knock on the doors of those people who voted in both the 1998 and 2000 Republican primary and general election. We put together walking-lists from our data-base. With a MAPSCO and a weekly calendar in hand, Daryl Irland and I meticulously plotted the streets and houses we would walk.

Almost every other evening for eight months, Daryl and I would meet in his parent's computer room and organize and print-out our weekly walking-lists. For hours upon hours, I would read off the streets of interest to Daryl and he would find the information in the database. He would then print the information and I would staple and organize the sheets. We easily went through a case of paper. We often got excited when there were multiple voter households on those lists. This meant that there were two, three, four, and sometimes more voters at that residence.

Daryl and I put together door-knocking teams. I had many young and energetic supporters. On a regular basis, Tiam Tavakoli, Josh Andor, John Hewitt, and Mary Matusik and her family walked door-to-door. There were others that occasionally walked with me door-to-door such as: John Binder, Syrous Malek, Amanda Housley, Tony Airhart, Aimee Johnson, Cindy Wheeler, and the late John Joshua.

Likewise, since I was very well-liked by the college population, I had many students who would just show up and help. Geoff Giordino, Claudia Taylor, Eman Afshar, Marjan Shansab, John Martin, and Jennifer Cruz would often show up for the weekend activities. During the week, however, it was just Daryl and I or just I walking door-to-door.

When Daryl and I went door-knocking it was always an experience. First, he would meet me either at my house or I would pick him up at his parent's house. We would jump in my Dodge 1500 pick-up truck and organize the walking list. By now, my truck had a huge 6' by 6' campaign sign in the back. As we proceeded to our walking destination, we would talk about anything and everything. Daryl and I bonded like family. And like family, we would often argue and then make up.

Daryl and I ate together quite frequently. One night after door-knocking, we decided to get some Chinese food. It was about 9:30pm, and the restaurant was nearly empty. We ordered our food, and even though it wasn't that good, we still ate all of it. We chatted about the evening and left right before they closed at 10:00pm.

On the drive to Daryl's house, almost simultaneously, we both started to have stomach pains. As we bantered about the cuisine, the pain got worse. We managed to make it to his house without having an accident. For the rest of the night and into the morning, we were both puking our guts out. We got food poising!

Daryl and I ate way too much on the campaign trail. After door knocking, we would stop and grab some take-out. Then we would both go home and eat dinner. When putting out signs at 2:00am, we would stop at various convenience stores and swallow down junk food such as doughnuts, cup-cakes, candy, and soda. Even though we were walking four to five miles a day, late night eating and consuming way too many calories, embarrassingly led to me to personally put on an extra forty pounds! Daryl probably gained about thirty pounds. It took me more than a year and a half to go from around 240 down to my current weight of 200 pounds.

Walking door-to-door isn't easy. With Daryl and I both working jobs, door-knocking became very tiresome. You must also be able to effectively communicate. When people would answer the door, I had an introductory speech memorized. Daryl and the other members of the door-knocking committee would say their own introduction.

Once people would answer the door, I would give them my introductory piece of literature. As they were looking at the literature, I would often say, "Hello, my name is Tom Caiazzo and I am running for U.S. Congress. I wanted to stop by and personally meet you and ask you to consider supporting me." I was always appropriately dressed and tried to look everyone in the eye. After the introduction, I always extended my hand and thanked them for their time. Initially, we got very positive feedback and almost every door we knocked on, people would engage in conversation and ask questions.

Daryl and I also implemented a policy of visiting the surrounding houses of those voter households on our list. Though many viewed this as a waste of time, we both thought that since we were right there, why not? Plus, this policy fell directly in-line with courting the new voter.

When going to these surrounding homes, I would always make sure to hand them voter registration cards. I would stress the importance of being registered, because if not, then they couldn't exercise their right to vote—or vote for me. I would also keep campaign yard signs in the back of my truck. Before leaving every house, I would ask both new voters and the voters on the list, if they would mind if I put a sign in their yard.

My yard signs had blue-lettering with a white background. It read "Caiazzo for Congress." My entire door-knocking committee must have put out 1500 yard signs. Combine that with my big 4 x 8 signs and Daryl's "homemade" plywood signs, I probably went through two-thousand signs. And guess who put most of them out?

With respect to the large signs, Daryl and I would leave my house about 11:00pm. We would drive to the busy intersections of the District and pound the metal stakes in the ground. We would then attach the sign. I would often call for permission to place the signs. I probably had more signs placed in the District than any other candidate running in the 2002 republican primary. Many of my signs also came up missing. My budget reflected this expenditure.

When we started door-knocking in early August, I had many supporters who wanted to help me knock on doors. The weather was hot, but we would walk in the evening hours. People would open their doors and say things like, "No candidate has ever knocked on my door before" and "I don't even know who my congressman is, but since you took time out to visit me, you have my support." Everyone in the campaign felt very confident. The strategy was working. And then 9/11 occurred.

I was sitting in my office preparing my lecture for my Tuesday American Government class when Janet called me. She said, "Are you following what is going on?" It was my birthday, so I shifted the conversation from what I thought was trivial to what she got me for my birthday. Janet said sternly, "Seriously, you need to watch the news. A commercial airplane just crashed into the World Trade Center."

As I left my office to find the closest television, a line of students were rushing to the Student Union to watch the news. I couldn't believe it.

On Tuesday, September 11, 2001 terrorists coordinated a series of attacks upon the United States. Predominantly targeting civilians, 19 men affiliated with Al-Qaeda hijacked four commercial passenger jet airliners. Each team of hijackers included a trained pilot. The pilots of two teams crashed two planes into the Twin Towers of the World Trade Center in New York City, one plane into each tower, causing both towers to collapse within two hours. The pilot of the third team crashed a plane into the Pentagon in Arlington County, Virginia. Passengers and members of the flight crew on the fourth hijacked aircraft attempted to retake control of their plane from the hijackers; that plane crashed into a field in rural Somerset County, Pennsylvania. Approximately 3,000 people died in these attacks.

After a week, Janet and I took an ad out in the local *Plano Star Courier* newspaper paper supporting the nation's commitment to fighting terrorism. The incumbent, who had been almost unseen for the last two years, became revitalized. Waving his POW flag and playing-up his military experience, the career politician was on every media outlet. People, who never heard of the Congressman, now did.

Due to the tragedy, we decided to post-pone door-knocking for about three weeks. When we resumed, things were different. Prior to 9/11, people were friendly and would open their doors. Not any more. You could literally tell that people were genuinely scared. But we plowed on. Though people didn't answer their doors as frequently, we still left them door-hangers. It was quite pathetic to often see people open their doors and take the hanger after we were down the block. Door-knocking would never be the same. Damn those terrorists.

Another grassroots strategy was to enter and be part of every major public event. With the abundance of college student support, I knew it was important to show that my candidacy was energetic, intelligent, and sincere; which was complete opposite of the incumbent. Using this support, the campaign made appearances at all the holiday events and parades.

During the Christmas season of 2001, the campaign made appearances at every tree lighting, ceremony, and parade. From the Christmas parade in the city of Wylie to the tree lighting in the city of Frisco, my campaign was making a presence. I felt it was so paramount to attend these public events.

One time, in error, we showed up at the city of Garland's tree lighting ceremony three days early! Josh, Tiam, Daryl and I seemed to be the only people in downtown Garland at 8:00pm. We made the best of it and ordered pizza at a local restaurant. They even let us put up a campaign sign in their window!

Even to this day, I am told that the "Caiazzo for Congress" campaign had the best turnout at parades. Parades are great for candidates to sit in their cars and wave to people for name/face identification. We decided to take it to another level. To reinforce the difference between the aging incumbent and myself, we wanted our entry to be energetic and personal. In every parade we entered in 2001 and 2002, we followed this theme. Two parades stand out.

The 4th of July, 2001 parade in the city of Plano kicked off our campaign. Out of all the political candidates, I had the most supporters. All of my Inner-Circle and their family, as well as about twenty college students and their friends, were in attendance. It was awesome. I remember Jeff, Jennie, and Sara Irland, Bill and Ladan Ardis, Zonk, and others. It was especially priceless when I saw other candidates stare in awe of my campaign's presence. I even recall the incumbent gawking at us. It felt good to see a look of concern on his face.

We had three vehicles decorated in campaign and patriotic memorabilia. With temperatures in the high 90s, I gave a pep talk to all and told them to go out and shake hands and pass out campaign shirts and literature. Unlike my opponent who sat in a car and waved, for a mile-and-a-half, I and all my supporters walked the parade route. There were literally four to five thousand people watching the parade. It seemed like I shook every hand. With our campaign song, "The Eye of the Tiger" blaring from my pick-up truck that a pregnant Janet was driving, people seemed to be in admiration of the energy and motivation.

The 2002 MLK parade in the city of Plano was equally unforgettable. Like my campaign did for every parade, we decorated the trucks and Daryl connected the speakers to my vehicle to play our campaign song. At least twenty or more supporters would be in attendance with campaign literature and shirts in hand. It was very windy and the temperature had to be in the low thirties. After checking in, I made small talk with MLK parade organizers. The incumbent congressman didn't bother to show-up. It wasn't expected because he had done nil nor ever expressed a concern for the African American community.

Though my supporters were cold, once the parade got under way, energy and enthusiasm was brewing from all in the campaign. Unfortunately, there were very few spectators. I am not sure if the weather played a role, but for a majority of the parade route I had more supporters walking the street than people actually watching the parade. After the end of the parade route, Darryl and I, as well as a few supporters, attended a MLK luncheon. Besides CCCC President Cary Israel, we were the only non-African American in attendance.

# One Month Before the Election

With the 2002 early voting dates slated from February 25 thru March 9th and Election Day itself Tuesday, March 12th, it was time to implement our "Thirty Day" strategy. Starting on January 25th, the campaign continued the grassroots approach, but we picked up the pace. We walked further and longer. It is estimated that come March 11th, we would have knocked on more than 15,000 doors. I must have personally knocked on at least 5,000.

Now was the right point to run our television commercial and radio spots. It was also time for telephone calls. Prior to these thirty days, our campaign made little to no telephone calls. I felt that door-knocking was more beneficial. There were some supporters, however, who felt uncomfortable walking door-to-door. They would rather call voters.

I am a believer that telephone calls aren't that effective. With the advent of caller-id, I felt that most people wouldn't answer their phone unless they knew who was calling. With telemarketers constantly calling people at inopportune times, I was very hesitant about this tactic.

Still, many in my Inner-Circle thought it was important to contact voters via the telephone. Jennie Irland took the leadership role. With a few lines at her home, supporters started making phone calls about thirty days before the election. I was advised that they received favorable responses. I was in high spirits.

It was also time to move the grassroots campaign beyond the cities of Plano and Allen. A few months earlier, the state legislature approved Texas' U.S. congressional districts. District 3's lines were clear. The cities of Garland, Rowlett and North Dallas were all in the District. Besides placing large campaign signs at busy intersections, I hadn't done any grassroots campaigning in those areas.

Starting the last week of January 2002, I decided to spend four straight Saturdays campaigning door-to-door in these areas. With a team of 6-8 supporters, we knocked from 10:00am to 4:00pm. Unfamiliar with the roads, it took a lot more time to find many of our streets.

I always supplied food and drink for the door-knockers. I recall one Saturday afternoon after campaigning all day in city of Rowlett when we stopped at the local Kentucky Fried Chicken. We had never seen an "All-u-Can-Eat" buffet offered at such establishment and we were hungry. About eight of us, lead by the hearty appetite of Daryl, ate almost everything on that buffet table. Josh, Tiam, Amanda and I laughed for almost an hour driving home, as I rocked the truck back-and-forth hoping to get Daryl to puke.

Champ Teng helped me garner a $1,000 donation from Born Lim. Born was an immigrant from Cambodia. Born worked hard to establish a very successful electronic manufacturing company in Dallas. Born and his family treated me with a tremendous amount of respect. He also respected Champ. With that $1,000, we would pay a flyer service to pass out 5,000 flyers in the Garland area the weekend before early voting.

Champ was a great asset to my campaign. He always thought that I should not worry about the grunt work of the campaign and focus on fundraising and meeting new people. With Champ, I attended many Asian festivities including an event at a Buddhist temple. Also, for the first time in my life I went into a Mosque. Let me state that these Muslims treated me with the utmost class and respect. They were some of the most compassionate and sincere folks I have ever met.

I attended every Asian-Indian event up to Election Day. With the support of friends from Pakistan, India, and Nepal, I was welcomed at all their events. One of my Asian-Indian supporters, Nick, called me one Saturday afternoon. I was knocking on doors in Rowlett. He said, "Tom, there are going to be 10,000 Asian-Indians at the Plano Centre tonight. It is a major political event with guest speaker, FBI Director, Robert Mueller. There will also be national and local television coverage. Be here today at 6:00pm, and I will pull some strings and get you to set-up a booth for free." I was all on it.

We left door-knocking about a half-hour early and I rushed home. Josh and Tiam agreed to go with me to the event. We changed and met at the Plano Cen-tre around 5:30pm. I found Nick and he let me set-up a booth in a prime loca-tion. The booth fee was $500, so indeed, Nick took care of me.

As the guest speakers started to parade on the platform, Nick's brother, Roger, grabs my arm and led me away from the booth. He says, "Tom, I pulled some strings and got you a place on the podium next to the FBI Director. You will also get a chance to say a few words." Though I was ecstatic, I was also unprepared. But, I had about ten minutes to come up with a three minute speech.

As I waited my turn, I chatted with Director Mueller. He was much taller than on TV, and a heck of a nice person. I was very impressed by his charm and poise. The emcee called my name and I went to the microphone. To say I was nervous was an understatement. I couldn't believe I was speaking in front of a 10,000+ people with a live TV broadcast. I was also unprepared and it showed in my speech. I was sweating from the lights. I used a lot of "Um" and "You Know" throughout the presentation. I concluded with passionately asking for their support. I received a decent applause.

Josh and Tiam said that I did "ok." Nick and Roger thought it went well. I was embarrassed. From that point on, I would always have a short generic speech memorized. I never spoke with note-cards, so I made sure to memorize that speech. I vowed to never be caught unprepared again.

I also went to a Deaf Club Celebration in Dallas. Grant Laird, the Director and friend, invited me to this event. Since I was committed to helping the deaf community, Grant gave me a free booth and access to many of the private events. I was a lot more prepared for this Sunday afternoon event.

The last thing for me to do was to organize poll workers. With some 30+ early voting and 100+ voting day precincts in the District, I wanted to have most of them staffed with volunteers. As people would come to vote, they would be met by a supporter holding my sign. They would greet the voter and ask them to consider voting for me. They would also hand each voter a "cheat sheet." This sheet would show people how to properly vote using a "puncher."

Early voting was quite easy to staff. Most of my Inner-Circle could handle these polls. I would personally work the early voting location at the College. Election Day, however, presented another challenge.

Since I was teaching American Government and had access to some 250 students, I decided to utilize these scholars. This was nothing new. As part of the college's commitment to service learning, I always offered students an opportunity to work in campaigns. I would even assign the work as part of the course evaluation or as an extra-credit opportunity. I never forced anyone into a specific campaign. I did the same with my election. I attained enough student support to cover almost 50% of the precinct for Election Day.

Some of my colleagues felt this was inappropriate and unethical. Prior to the start of the semester, I consulted with President Cary Israel. He said it would be fine as long as I don't force them to work in my campaign. I also consulted with my senior political science colleague, Dr. Loren Miller. He concurred with President Israel's statement.

I think this would be an appropriate time for me to discuss some of my CCCC colleagues' behavior toward me and my campaign. One would think that every colleague, no matter what their party affiliation, would support my political pursuit. To my embarrassment, that wasn't the case. It was upsetting to hear from students that other professors were talking in a negative manner toward me and my campaign. In fact, of the forty-plus people in my Social Sciences division, only Loren Miller gave me a campaign contribution. And he did it twice!

Besides Loren Miller, there were only a handful of other colleagues at my academic institution that either attended my campaign events or even gave me verbal support. It seemed like many were jealous of my endeavor. Some wouldn't even talk to me about it. It was sad.

I will never forget the Friday after the 9/11 tragedy. Jon Hewitt, the President of the College Republicans, wanted me to inquire about the Club organizing a "Prayer at the Pole." Simultaneously, the President of the United States, George W. Bush, declared that same day the "National Day of Prayer." I helped organize the event and it was advertised throughout the community.

Unbeknownst to me, many of the college faculty felt that the prayer was inappropriate. As the prayer activities were going on, I recall one Atheist political science faculty member sadly spouting, "Why, Why?" Another Jewish faculty member specifically approached me and wanted to know why the minister concluded the prayer with "in the name of Jesus."

I consider myself a major civil libertarian. I am a major advocate for the separation of church and state, and don't want government interfering with one's religion or even engaging in policy making. I know full-well that the free exercise and establishment clauses of the First Amendment guarantee the right to practice one's religion free of government interference. For some professors to object to a prayer organized by "students" and to be attended "voluntarily," however, is blatantly asinine.

As a political science professor for the past fifteen years, I can unequivocally say that I was stunned by the antics and behavior of my colleagues. The back-stabbing, innuendos, and rumors were inappropriate and unprofessional. I am sad to say that the faculty, who preach and teach civic engagement, didn't even participate in my or other political campaigns. Some didn't even vote.

I do, however, want to thank the CCCC faculty and staff members who did assist my campaign by either signing my petition, attending a fundraiser, or for just being supportive. I sincerely value the efforts of: Dr. Cary Israel; Dr. Loren Miller; Dr. Bill Adler; Dr. Sirous Malek; Tony Airhart; Marty Berryman; Jim Sigona; Greg Dennis; Tim Peters; Dr. Matt Coulter; Sharon Art; Bill McCracken; Karen Knapp; Mary Wright; Kim Kramer; Omri Crewe; Miguel Alacarn; Marti Miles-Rosenfield; Kevin Henard; Chuck Lalanne; Chris Sampson; Aimee Johnson; Ed Leathers; Nick Geller; Linda Adams; Craig Leverette; Pam Gaiter; Doug Dunlap; Bill and Ladan Ardis; Larry Collins; Dr. Bob Forester; Dr. Peggy Brown; Ann Yeargan; Jill Whitston; Rex Parcells; Linda Adams; Walt Nilsen; Rebecca Crowell; Andy Sharpe; Eric Donihoo; and, the late John Joshua. I am sure there are others, but these specific friends need to be recognized.

I was equally stunned by the poor support from local area teachers. Though I attained favorable comments from them while door-knocking, very few openly supported my candidacy. My campaign asked for endorsements from various teacher groups, and we didn't get any. Though the crux of my campaign was improving funding for education, not one elementary or high school teacher gave me a campaign contribution.

About two weeks before the election, I found out that the largest Protestant church in the District was hosting a candidate "Meet and Greet." Since churches aren't supposed to engage in politics, they were careful how to advertise and word the event. I wasn't invited to the event, even though my opponent was going to be in attendance. My Inner-Circle called the church and requested reciprocity. Jon Hewitt played my commercial to the crowd and Jennie Irland staffed the table. The pastor ended the event by saying, though not directly, to support the career congressman; so much for the separation of church and state.

Though the media coverage was light and I was ostracized by the party, the campaign moved forward. Following the strategy to "Shock the World," I had hope. The campaign had hope. We believed that the citizens of the District never participated or became civically engaged, because they didn't have a choice or a voice. Our campaign worked very hard to give the people hope. With thirty days to go, I was doing everything possible to not let them down.

# Early Voting and Election Day

The weekend before early voting, Jennie Irland held a late Sunday afternoon gathering at her home. There were about twelve people in attendance. Daryl and I showed up after door-knocking. We had a nice cookout. We also prepared for early voting.

In the state of Texas, registered voters may vote early at a location convenient to them within their political subdivision. Early voting in person starts seventeen days before each election and ends four days before each election.

The night before early voting, Daryl and I placed campaign signs at all the early voting polling locations. We started about 7:00pm and didn't get through until 4:00am. As we worked all night long, we didn't see any other candidates doing the same thing. At the Garland location, we ran into this nice man who was putting out a bunch of political campaign signs for different candidates. He was being paid to do this service. And he was also putting signs out for my career opponent.

Since three of the early voting polling locations were at the various campuses of Collin County Community College (CCCC), I was very optimistic about early voting. With 12,000-plus students at the Spring Creek campus (Plano) alone, I was going to spend most of my time at this location. Other members of my Inner-Circle would staff the additional locations throughout the District. Janet and I voted early at the Spring Creek campus. We also brought Dante. At the ripe age of two months, we helped him ceremoniously cast his first vote for his daddy.

Before and after class, I would greet and meet students and ask them to vote. Though the poll was right in the middle of the campus atrium, voter turnout was low. I figured that student's would be voting in droves. They weren't. I worked harder to get people to vote, and at times, even grabbing students I knew and walking them to the poll.

I would call all my supporters and ask them how things were going. The answer was always the same: "Things are looking good, but voter turnout is low." I was getting worried. For me to upset the incumbent, I was expecting a very high voter turnout. A low turnout favors the incumbent. Still, we pushed on and remained positive.

About 10:30am, Angelo DiSalvo called me. Angelo, my friend and WWII veteran, told me that a poll worker at the city of Allen precinct told him to vote for the incumbent instead of me. I was shocked! Angelo said, "I couldn't see the ballot too well. I asked the lady to help me vote. As I was voting and got to the U.S. Congress race, I told her I wanted to vote for Tom Caiazzo. I was told to vote for Sam Johnson. I was furious and have no clue if I punched the right name or not!"

As you can imagine, I was infuriated. I had heard from some others that these voting irregularities were occurring at a few other precincts as well. After the 2,000 presidential fiasco in Florida, anything was possible. So, I quickly contacted Sharon Rowe in the Elections Office. She contacted the poll worker and they denied Angelo's story, as well as other allegations. She reminded me that all her workers were well trained. I pressed her to double-check all these claims. She agreed.

When early voting ended, we spent the final weekend prior to Election Day walking door-to-door. My few television and radio ads were running. Flyers were mailed to voters in Garland. Some supporters were making last minute phone calls. We were doing everything we could to win this election.

The afternoon before the Election Day, Daryl and I went out and placed campaign signs at almost every polling precinct. After my Monday classes, we hit the road. I brought a change of clothes because I knew I wouldn't get home until two days later. I was right. We spent all afternoon Monday and early am Tuesday putting out signs.

During this time, my cell phone was ringing every five minutes. Mary and Jennie were coordinating poll workers and trying to get everything organized for Election Day. Daryl and I finished putting out all the signs around 5:00 am, Tuesday morning. We met up with Mary at the local IHOP. In two hours, the polls would open. It was show-time. It was time to see if we were indeed going to "Shock the World."

After breakfast, I took Daryl home. He was designated to be the campaign "runner." He would float back and forth to each poll checking on workers. He would provide workers with drinks, food, campaign materials, answer questions, etc. Also, Mary left to work a poll by her house. She also started to call the other poll workers to make sure everyone was in place.

I paid the breakfast bill and called Janet. We chatted about the big day and she knew that no matter what would happen today, I had campaigned with integrity and honesty. I gave Dante a kiss over the phone and headed to Dallas County. The committee thought it would be good for me to have a presence at the polls in Dallas County on Election Day. I agreed. After washing-up and changing at a local convenience store, I psyched myself up for the biggest and most important day in my campaign life.

Tuesday, March 12th, 2002 will go down for me as a day in infamy. Though I hadn't slept in days, I was full of energy and enthusiasm. I was very optimistic and knew no matter what, I had worked my tail off.

When the polls opened, I started to get concerned. There were no long lines. Of the few people voting, most of them seemed to be over the age of sixty. This wasn't good. Still, I figured it was early and most young and new voters would be voting on their lunch hour or after work. I was so wrong. Voter turnout for the entire day was pathetic. I could literally count on my hands the number of people voting in some polling locations.

I spent the next nine hours campaigning at every polling precinct in Dallas County. The voter turnout was low at each location. I tried to remain optimistic and convinced myself that we won the election based on early voting.

It was getting dark, so I left the Garland City Hall polling location and headed to a school in Rowlett. On the way there, Daryl calls me. He is screaming that he is lost and can't find the rural polling precincts in the cities if Murphy and Wylie. Though Daryl didn't find it funny, I was cracking up. We both started laughing as well. I love that young man and could not have survived the campaign with him. At this point of the campaign, we needed to laugh. It was great medicine. As I guided him to the various locations, I asked him about voter turnout. Daryl's answer was the same that I was getting from every poll worker: "low!" When the polls closed at 7:00pm, I headed back to Plano.

During the forty-five minute drive, I worked the phone to check on everyone. I called Jon Hewitt to make sure he was at the Election's Office. Jon was our point-man to both monitor the counting and call us with the results. I also called Mary. Mary opened her home for our "Victory Party." She said everything was in order, and the forty pizzas that the local "Angelo and Vito's" Pizzeria donated, had been delivered. Janet and Dante were already at Mary's house, as well as some of the poll workers.

I arrived at the party around 7:50pm. Everyone was in great spirits and having a grand time. I was greeted by all and went directly to see Janet and Dante. I hugged and kissed them. I then embraced Mary, Daryl, and Jennie. We had all worked so hard. I was starving and must have eaten an entire pizza in about ten minutes.

About 8:10pm, Daryl tells me that Jon is on the phone. I asked Daryl the news. He said, "I don't know. Jon wants to talk to you." I said, "Ok, Jon. Give me the results from the early voting." In a saddened tone Jon said, "Sam got 75% and you have 25%." To say I was displeased would be an understatement. Jon said a few other things, but I wasn't paying attention. I said to Jon, "Ok, call me when you get some of the precinct results."

Daryl saw the look in my eyes and was disappointed. I immediately told Janet and my Inner-Circle. Sensing everyone was down, I tried to cheer all up with a brief speech about how we still had the Election Day votes and anything is possible. Mary joined in and told everyone to eat and drink, and have a great time.

I slipped into the bathroom to wash my face. I knew the election was over. Since Election Day voter turnout was so low, there was no way for me to catch up. Sure enough, Jon calls me back with the depressing results. It was worse, with about 70% of the precincts in, the incumbent had 80% of the vote. I told Jon there was no need for him to stay at the Election's Office any more, and to come to the party. The final results from my race were 84.3% for the incumbent and 15.7% for me.

The phone rang again and this time it was the Dallas Morning News. They asked me for a comment about the results. I gave them some magnanimous generic reply. I wanted to give them a profanity laced diatribe, but thought otherwise, A few minutes later, I asked Mary to gather everyone in the living room for a speech. I told my supporters the results. I stressed that we worked hard and gave the incumbent a battle. I reminded them that though we lost, we still won. We brought many people into the system and that they now need to continue to stay engaged. I closed with again thanking all for their support.

Almost simultaneously, Miguel Alacarn called everyone's attention. With tears flowing, Miguel thanked me for running and for everyone's hard work. He reminded us that the first time is always the most difficult, and that next time the results will be different. I hugged Miguel and everyone seemed upbeat.

Before leaving to go home, I remember pulling Jon Hewitt to the side. Jon was very upset from the loss. I reminded Jon that he worked his tail off and he has nothing to be sad about. I said the same things to a few others who were down such as Daryl Irland, Josh Andor, and Tiam Tavakoli.

After being up now for some fifty-hours, it was nice to go home and get some sleep. But as you could imagine, I slept very little. With my mind racing one-hundred miles per hour, I eventually settled down and grabbed a few hours of sleep. In a way I was relieved that it was all over. I could now spend more time with my family.

I woke up at 7:00am to go to my Wednesday class. Once I arrived at the office, I decided to go online and view the official results. As I viewed the numbers, it was obviously clear why the incumbent won: voter turnout was only 4.6%! I couldn't believe that after all the hard work by me and my campaign, nearly 95% of the population didn't vote. A closer examination of the empirical data showed that very few new voters participated in the primary. Operation "Shock the World" was a failure.

# Conclusion

A few months after the primary election, I was approached by a few political science scholars regarding my congressional campaign. They wanted to know if my campaign was to "win" or simply to lay the ground work for name identification and a future run when the incumbent opts to retire. The same questions were asked by the media. My answer was and is still the same: it was a campaign of hope. The hope for those who are disgruntled. The hope that they would channel their dissatisfaction at the ballot box. The hope that they would elect someone with energy, ideas, and integrity. It was a campaign about new blood and new ideas. It was a campaign to win for not only myself or the community, but for the nation and our political system in general. It was about hope for all.

If you recall, I made it unequivocally clear at the first meeting with my Inner-Circle that the "Shock the World" strategy would either lead us to victory or get us thumped. Unfortunately, it was the latter.

I wasn't stupid and I had some idea how campaigns worked; especially one against an entrenched incumbent. It should be noted, however, the campaign strategy might have strategically been a failure, but tactically we were successful. I would say very successful.

What congressional campaign could have sustained for more than a year on a budget of less than $14,000? Unlike my opponent who had nearly $1 million, we operated on a shoe string budget. And we still covered the basics such as: radio and TV ads, campaign flyers and literature, and campaign signs.

We also stayed focused on the objective at hand. For almost eight months, we walked door-to-door, attended parades, and had a presence at community events. We garnered supporters and registered people to vote. I campaigned in an ethical and positive manner. We courted racial and ethnic minorities, and tried to woo Democrats.

And I did all of this with political novices. There were no professionals per se. My campaign had men and woman who believed in me and my ideals. They had energy and enthusiasm, and a will that was unmatched. Jon Hewitt, Josh Andor, Tiam Tavokoli, Jennie and Jeff Irland, and Mary Matusik and her family labored for almost a year. And make no mistake about it, besides my wife and son, Daryl Irland was an inspiration to my campaign. His diligence and commitment to the campaign for a college sophomore is unprecedented.

I challenge anyone to show me a congressional campaign which operated in such a diligent manner on our budget. If anything, my campaign needs to be commended for their commitment to the strategy in light of all the adversity and obstacles. This is especially true after 9/11.

Moreover, I will admit that the campaign strategy was indisputably a failure. My congressional campaign proved that you can't win an election against a career incumbent based on "hope." We hoped that new voters would turnout in droves. We hoped that a lot of racial and ethnic minorities would participate. We hoped that the local Democratic Party would get its members to cross-over and vote for me. We hoped to get a tremendous amount of media coverage. We hoped that educators would participate in droves. We hoped wrong.

In retrospect, I believe that prior to 9/11/2001, my campaign was on the right track. If I could turn back the clock, however, I would do many things different. First and foremost, I should have never run without the support of the local party and/or a plethora of money. I cared and thought way too much of the common person. The masses didn't give a hoot, and even though I tried, they resorted back to their apathy and ignorance. The 90% of the population have no sense of political efficacy.

Even though I cared, they didn't. Due to this reality, I now see why money is so important in elections—especially at the national level. I guess Shakespeare was right when he said the only things people care about are "bread and circuses."

Second, I should have dropped out after the 9/11 catastrophe. I had no idea that the worst terrorist act in the history of the United States would occur during my campaign. Until that event, everything seemed like it was working and the grassroots campaigning was making a difference. Once 9/11 happened, like a phoenix, the incumbent milked the event to his advantage. He parlayed his military service and POW status to calm the electorate.

Lastly, I should have accepted the offer from Richard Dotson to run for State Representative against the incumbent. After all my hard work, I felt like myself and the entire campaign was cheated. We were never taken seriously. We didn't have any support from the local party. We didn't get any major donations. If I would have aligned myself with Mr. Dotson, I would have had all the aforementioned.

I understand why candidates have to raise hundreds of thousands of dollars. They need to convince the less than ten percent of the population to turn-out and vote for them. If one has the unlimited resources to advertise, run radio and TV ads, and constantly bombard people with information, this continual inundation may influence folks to vote. Until Congress passes sensible campaign finance reform, which probably won't be in my lifetime, money will still rule elections at the state and federal level.

As such, based on the demographics and reality of our contemporary society, operation "Shock the World" can only be an effective campaign strategy if a candidate has a plethora of money and support from the political party. The people have let this system be taken over by the special interests. If one puts their hopes in the hands of the masses, they will undeniably fail.

This is the greatest nation in the world. We have the best political system. However, this great Republic can only survive if the people participate. Our representative democracy depends upon the people being active, aware, engaged, and involved. Most people could care less and they have, in essence, let the system down and lost all hope.

# Epilogue

It is 2007 and I frequently think about my 2002 Congressional campaign. I now spend my time, however, trying to be a good husband to Janet and an even better father to Dante.

I am teaching political science at East Georgia College. I continually strive for excellence in the classroom. East Georgia College is a stellar institution of higher education and it's President Dr. John Black, my Chair, Dr. David Bartram, and all my colleagues and staff is extremely professional and scholarly. This intellectual environment offers me the opportunity to advance in my discipline while trying innovative educational techniques in the classroom.

I am also still energetic in the community and neighborhood. A few neighbors and I recently mobilized the community to prevent a cell phone tower from being built about 300' from our backyards. Don't mess with the power of the people! I may run for a local office in the near future, and who knows about another congressional run.

I know that the world has changed a lot since 9/11/2001. But I still reflect and wonder "what if I was elected." With respect to the issues, if I had won Congress, my ideology and vote would be based on my best judgment. I wouldn't be owned by the special interest groups. I would be my own man and do what is right. A lot of my issues and ideas haven't been co-opted or addressed by either the Democrats or Republicans. We are the greatest nation in the world but we are capable of so much more. Our children deserve nothing less. But I categorically and unequivocally believe that this country needs immediate reform.

For example: It is unconditionally clear that teachers at all levels are under-appreciated, underpaid, and undervalued; Elementary, secondary, and higher education still needs massive reform; Wages aren't increasing to match the levels of inflation and the cost of living; Though some people have insurance and the government is picking up the tab, everyone doesn't have adequate health care coverage. All people need to have access to affordable health insurance; Unilateral foreign policy is ineffective and multilateral cooperation with the U.N. is our best defense against terrorism in the global world; To eliminate career politicians, Term Limits need to be invoked; With the national debt close to $10 trillion, we need a constitutional amendment to mandate a balanced budget; Combine the aforementioned while ending bureaucratic waste and fraudulent spending, and then, and only then, will we get our economy under control; We need to give the large oil companies tax incentives to move away from fossil fuels and be the leaders in finding alternative energy and fuel sources; We need to protect all ten of the Bill of Rights, not just the second. Freedom of religion and expression needs to be allowed and government has no right to infringe upon these liberties; Common sense policymaking such as road construction at night, defending our borders, tax breaks for the middle-class, and empowering the poor; Show all people, no matter what their race or class status, an abundance of compassion and care; Equality for people with disabilities; Practical environmental policies to maintain our ecosystem; and, Protecting Social Security and Medicare for the elderly.

If I do run for any local, state, or federal office, the strategy will also be different. Because of the impact of terrorism, the "Shock the World" strategy is not plausible. If I run for office two things must happen: 1) I need to have the support of the local political party; and, 2) I need to have more money than my opponent. There is no room to compromise. Though Dr. Martin Luther King said, "Everything that is done in the world is done by hope," I disagree. When it comes to politics, it is all about money and the support of the political party. Stay tuned. I can always be found throughout the world by accessing my website at: http://www.tomcaiazzo.com. God Bless you, your family, and the United States of America!

www.ingramcontent.com/pod-product-compliance
Lightning Source LLC
Chambersburg PA
CBHW021824270326
41932CB00007B/326